# The Richer Woman

A woman's guide to true wealth

## Omilola Oshikoya

© 2017 Omilola Oshikoya

ISBN: 978-978-959-173-2 (*Amazon Edt*)

Scripture quotations marked (NLT) are taken from the Holy Bible, New Living Translation, copyright © 1996, 2004, 2007 by Tyndale House Foundation. Used by permission of Tyndale House Publishers, Inc., Carol Stream, Illinois 60188. All rights reserved.

Scripture quotations marked (ESV) are from the ESV® Bible (The Holy Bible, English Standard Version®), copyright © 2001 by Crossway, a publishing ministry of Good News Publishers. Used by permission. All rights reserved.

Scripture quotations marked (NIV) are from THE HOLY BIBLE, NEW INTERNATIONAL VERSION®, NIV® Copyright © 1973, 1978, 1984, 2011 by Biblica, Inc.® Used by permission. All rights reserved worldwide.

Scripture quotations marked (NKJV) taken from the New King James Version®. Copyright © 1982 by Thomas Nelson. Used by permission. All rights reserved.

Scripture quotations marked (MEV) Scripture taken from the Modern English Version. Copyright © 2014 by Military Bible Association. Used by permission. All rights reserved.

Scripture quotations marked (MSG) taken from *The Message*. Copyright © 1993, 1994, 1995, 1996, 2000, 2001, 2002. Used by permission of NavPress Publishing Group."

Scripture quotations marked (WEB) take from The World English Bible (WEB) a Modern English translation of the Holy Bible and is in the Public Domain.

**ALL RIGHTS RESERVED.** This book contains material protected under International and Federal Copyright Laws and Treaties. Any unauthorized reprint or use of this material is prohibited. No part of this book may be reproduced or transmitted in any form or by any means, electronic or mechanical, including photocopying, recording, or by any information storage and retrieval system without express written permission of the publisher, except in the case of brief quotations embodied in critical reviews and certain noncommercial uses permitted by copyright law.

# Dedication

This book is dedicated to my best friend, my lover, my husband and the father of my children, John Olugbenga Oshikoya. You are everything and everything is you. You are the Richer man.

This book is dedicated to my daughters Oluwaferanmi and Oluwafiorehanmi. May you become Richer Women and marry Richer Men.

This book is dedicated to my son Olaoluwaloseyi, may you become the Richer man and marry and help your wife become the Richer Woman.

This book is also dedicated to every woman who would like to live a life of purpose. It is also dedicated to every woman with a story or a past who feels unworthy and believes they have nothing to offer the world. God can and will use anyone.

This book is also dedicated to Oluwatosin, a woman who lived a life of purpose.

*"Teach us to number our days so that we can apply our heart to wisdom."*
**Psalm 90:12 (NKJV)**

# Table of Contents

Dedication     3

Foreword     9

## Part 1: The Rich Woman

A Moth or A Butterfly, Which Would You Rather Be?     13

All That Glitters     17

The Broken Little Girl     23

The Lady and Her Quest For Love     27

The One     35

My Career vs. My Marriage     41

Tests and Trials     45

Doing it Afraid     55

Falling Into Temptation     59

Beauty For Ashes     69

The Biggest Do-It-Afraid Moment of my Life     75

The Birth of This Book     83

# Part 2: The Richer Woman

## Who is the Richer Woman? — 89

## Role as the Father's Daughter — 95
- Who Is The Father? — 95
- The Father's Daughter — 97
- The Father's Love — 99
- The Father's Single Daughter — 100
- The Fathers daughter and the sunflower — 103
- God's Purpose for His Married Daughters — 106

## Role as a wife — 111
- Purpose — 114
- Love and Sex — 119
- Finances — 121
- Prayer — 124
- Choosing a Husband — 125

## Role as a Mother — 129
- True Success: The Olive Tree. — 130
- Ensuring Your Child's Success — 134

## Components of the Richer Woman — 143
- Spirituality — 145
- Family — 153
- Work/Career/Achievements — 157
- Health and Wellbeing — 167
- Friendships/Relationships — 171
- Fun/Recreation/Rest — 179
- Money/Finances — 183
- Time Management — 197

## Why People Don't Become the Richer Woman — 201
- What is Fear? — 201
- Fear Of Failure: — 203
- Fear Of Trading Security For The Unknown — 205
- Fear of what others would say or think. — 206
- Fear Of Not Being Able To Cope Financially — 208

## Be The Richer Woman: Do It Afraid — 213
- Have Vision — 214

| | |
|---|---|
| *Change Your Belief System* | *215* |
| *Believe In Yourself And Believe In Your Dreams* | *217* |
| *Do It Now* | *219* |
| *Take the first step without knowing what lies ahead* | *219* |
| *Build A Dream Team* | *221* |
| *Stay Motivated* | *222* |
| *Stay grateful* | *223* |
| *Trust The Process* | *224* |

## Acknowledgements 231

## About the Author 237

# Foreword

My husband and I read the draft copy of the Richer Woman that was sent to us with a mixture of excitement and apprehension. Excitement, because of the candour and realness of the content – and the balm we knew it would be for many for that very reason – and apprehension, for the same reason. We wondered if sharing so much would make Omilola vulnerable to attack. But I sat back on completion, really awed and inspired by her courage. I realise her personal story and journey is critical to the healing power of this book. It's this dangerous vulnerability that is so powerful. Even in 2017, it's rare, especially in Christian circles, to experience this level of truth. In John 8:32, Jesus said '.... the truth will set you free'. I believe Omilola's truth will set many free.

From the initial details of her fledging love life in secondary school days to the more tumultuous university romance, and then onto meeting the man who would be her husband, we see the lessons she needed to learn unfolding through the choices she makes, and we see the consequences that follow. We see how her brokenness drove her to make poor relationship choices and to build a career that robbed her family life, and we see God's redeeming grace woven in as 'Mr Mysterious' arrives on the scene. We see how as frustrations, accidents and God's whispers lead her into a career of purpose. We learn that, far from being just a funky slogan, 'Do it Afraid' is something she's lived. It's been both a springboard into purpose and a continual source of challenge to reach higher and do better.

Don't be fooled! While this is an 'equipping book' – skilling you, especially in part C, to fulfill potential – its central message is about much more than career prominence and success; it is also about growing into a godly wife and mother, and discovering yourself as a unique human being and an object of divine love. It's about learning to love yourself and discover your unique path through this world. It's a story of discovering God, growing in God and walking with God.

The book's conversational style is endearing and enchanting. It ropes you in, like the aromas wafting out of a candy store draw you in as you walk by, and delivers truth in a sweet and accessible manner. I know this book will make you chuckle, reflect on your life, reconsider your priorities and provoke your faith. Then Omilola's goal will be realized: to challenge you to start your journey to becoming the Richer woman God made you to be.

Are you ready? Fasten your seat belt and enjoy the ride. We are off to a great destination!

**Bimbo Fola-Alade**

*Co-Lead Pastor*, The Liberty Church, London

*Bimbo Fola-Alade started professional life as a lawyer. She is now a well regarded bible teacher, pastor and conference speaker; and has a strong mentoring ministry to young adults and women. She has over 20 years of ministry experience in the area of marriage, relationships and life issues for women and singles. She has written six books and is married to Pastor Sola Fola-Alade of the Liberty Church, London and they have two teenage sons.*

# PART 1
# *The Rich Woman*

# A Moth or A Butterfly, Which Would You Rather Be?

At one point in my life, my main goal and aspiration in life was to be rich and successful. Money, for me, was the answer to everything; if I could be rich then I would be happy, I would gain respect and be loved by all.

Let us take a look at the definition of rich:

According to Oxford dictionary, the word 'rich' can be defined as 'having a great deal of money or assets; wealthy.'

As I have grown in my relationship with God, and through life experiences, I have come to realise that, contrary to popular opinion, there is a difference between being 'rich' and being 'wealthy', and there is a difference between the word 'rich' and the word 'richer'.

True wealth consists of more than money. Money is only one aspect of wealth, and it is more expedient to have true wealth than money.

The analogy of the Moth and the Butterfly will make this clearer.

The Moth and the Butterfly are very similar insects. They share the same physical structure and the same process of metamorphosis – where they are transformed from crawling caterpillars into flying insects – and yet, they are different.

Many writers and speakers have used the caterpillar's process of metamorphosis as an analogy to describe the painful process human beings must go through in life, in order to become better. They use this analogy to encourage their audiences to hold on to the process because, very soon, they will evolve into something "beautiful".

These speakers usually refer to the process where the caterpillar evolves into a Butterfly, but rarely do they use the moth in this analogy. They have failed to highlight that it is possible to go through this same painful process and evolve into a not-so-beautiful Moth.

Let's look at a few of the differences between Butterflies and Moths:

| Moth | Butterfly |
| --- | --- |
| Active at night | Active during the day |
| Attracted to artificial light | Attracted to sunlight |
| Rest with their wings tented down | Rest with their wings folded up |
| Usually dull coloured | Vivid coloured |
| Over 100,000 species | Circa 15,000 species |

By looking at the differences alone it is clear that, while the Butterfly and the Moth have similar physical appearances, they have opposing behavioural characteristics.

The Butterfly comes out during the day and can see the beauty of the earth. It also receives its energy from the true source of light and warmth – the sun. The Moth, on the other hand, comes out at night and is restricted to artificial light (such as light bulbs) in order to stay warm and have energy for flight.

But of all these differences, one profound thing that stuck out to me is the fact that there are significantly more Moths than Butterflies. For every ten Moths, there're only one or two Butterflies.

God revealed to me that there are two types of people on earth. There are people who live their lives as Moths, and people who live their lives as Butterflies. Sadly, like the statistics of the Moth and the Butterfly, most people live life as Moths while very few live life as Butterflies.

The Moth represents most people: people who live life working in careers that they do not like, people who desire to be rich at the expense of their children, marriages, family, their health, and even eternity – people who live the 'Rich life'.

The Butterfly represents people who live full and content lives. They are purpose-driven. They live the 'Richer life'.

A 'Rich Woman' can be considered a Moth, while 'The Richer Woman' can be considered a Butterfly.

I once lived my life like a Moth, literally speaking. I used to leave the house early in the morning, when it was still dark, and get back home late at night when it was dark. Like the Moth, I was active at night.

A lot of the time, my children would be in bed by the time I returned home and I never got to spend time with them.

My Moth lifestyle also affected my marriage; I was attracted to artificial things, also known as the 'finer things of life', and it was all about making money and being rich and successful.

I wasn't happy, I wasn't fulfilled; my 'light' didn't shine, and the true extent of my beauty was hidden. I didn't get to experience life in its grandeur.

Like both insects, I also went through metamorphosis. I went through painful processes and paid my dues, but what is the point of paying your dues only to end up as a Moth, when you can make the same sacrifice and become a Butterfly?

Thankfully, I have chosen to be a Butterfly and no longer live the life of a Moth.

A Moth or a Butterfly, which would *you* rather be?

For most people, the answer to this question is obvious. But if the Butterfly is the obvious answer, why doesn't every woman choose to be a Butterfly?

My story will provide some insight.

# All That Glitters

My earliest memories of childhood are of boat rides, beach trips and picnics, my dad teaching us to swim, and the grand Sunday lunches my mum would prepare every week. In those days, we were only allowed chicken and sodas on Sundays and I relished those meals for the chance to indulge. Sometimes we would visit my grandma at her home, eating her signature 'gurudi' coconut biscuits, or we would spend time at the luxurious Sheraton Hotel.

We lived in the lovely GRA in Ikeja, where we had the luxury of serene streets where we could ride our bicycles in safety. We never lacked friends, because we were constantly surrounded by cousins who were like sisters, and everything was rosy. My dad was my hero, and he still is. I thought he was the strongest person in the world, I thought he could fight and beat anyone up! My mum was, and still is, my angel. As the only girl in a family of three, we share a strong bond. She's the most beautiful woman I know. I was always excited whenever she picked me up from school, so I could show her off. The boys in school would swoon over my mum, an absolutely stunning woman with long hair and fair skin. In fact, that was one of the reasons I didn't like my complexion when I was younger, I wanted to be fair, just like my beautiful mum.

My mum taught me about Jesus. We would sit and read the Bible together. She would always take us to one prayer meeting or church program or the other. She always had meetings from one society to the other after church, and we would have to sit and wait what seemed like hours for her to finish!

My mum also took us with her whenever she was going to visit the poor. She has such a huge heart. Once, when we were on our way out, there was a ghastly accident on the bridge. My mum stopped her car to help out, and we even went to the house of the deceased to break the news to the family.

There's a wide gap between my older brother and I; by the time I was five, he was already in boarding school! But my younger brother and I are close in age and so we grew up together and became very close. We fought a lot growing up, but we loved – and still love – each other very much.

And yet, with these wonderful memories, there was an unpleasant side to my childhood.

When I was around 6 years old, my grandfather died. He had been one of the wealthiest men in his generation. Through the company he founded, he was the sole producer and supplier of cement bags for all the cement companies in the country. This was just one of his many investments, his portfolio also included one of the oldest newspapers in Nigeria. He was a philanthropist and a very influential man in his time, and my father had worked for him.

When my grandfather passed away, all the wealth we had enjoyed followed suit. His company eventually had to be shut down, and none of the business ventures my dad tried on his own worked out. We had a roof over our heads for the majority of the time, but things were tough.

It didn't help that we were in one of the most expensive schools in Nigeria at the time; most of our classmates came from very affluent homes, and I was always afraid that our names would be included in the list of students owing fees.

I detested resumption after summer holidays. Most of our classmates – who would have travelled abroad for the holidays – would return with stories and fancy new things that we couldn't afford. The last time I remembered travelling was when I was about five and I would pray every year that we would get the chance to travel for summer.

Once, when I was diagnosed with a stomach ulcer, I told my dad that the doctors said it was because I had been worrying too much! I so desperately wanted to go abroad like all my rich friends, that my mind was completely preoccupied with the idea.

He must have felt obligated to find a way to make it happen, particularly since my older brother had been sent to school abroad by my aunt. And, in the end, my father borrowed to send me to university abroad.

I am very grateful for the opportunity to have gone abroad. It was very expensive and he did it to make me happy, but at the same time it was really difficult being broke and without my immediate family in a different country.

I took on whatever jobs I could find while in university, including a cleaning job, as pocket money was not constant. Once, I didn't have any money to eat, so I slept more than 24 hours straight just so that I wouldn't have to feel the hunger. I would wake up and force myself to go back to sleep. I was afraid of rejection, so I could never ask for help.

Once, I returned to school from a trip to London (my school was outside London). I didn't have any money on me but it was fine, since the last coach usually stopped on the University Campus. It was late at night and I slept off, so I didn't hear the driver ask if anyone was going to the University, and he drove straight to town.

When I woke up and realized what had happened, I was afraid because I didn't have any money to get back to school and it was really late. By God's grace, I had 10 pence on me and I was able to use the payphone to call a friend. She told me to take a cab to her dormitory and paid for me.

One summer, I had worked so hard that I was excited to have earned some good money. It wasn't going to be a bad term after all – or so I thought, but one of my aunts, who helped pay my fees whenever my dad couldn't, asked me how much I had saved. I was afraid because I hadn't really saved much, my plan had been to fall back on my overdraft. I told her I had a thousand pounds and she told me I had to use it to pay my fees, which I did.

I honestly can't remember how I survived that term. Sometimes I would be so broke, and then out of nowhere, someone at church would invite me over for lunch without knowing I desperately needed that invitation. I truly had some of the best people around me.

Back home in Nigeria, due to the financial pressures, my dad always threatened to sell or rent out our house. Many times, people would walk into our house to view the property while we were there. On one occasion, he rented it out and rented a smaller house for us to live in. This made financial sense because there was no point living in a big, unfinished house while we were struggling cash-wise. And it was fine until the landlord of the house we were renting decided he wanted to sell his house. We couldn't afford to buy it, we couldn't afford rent for another property and our own house had been rented out.

Eventually, the house was sold. I had to go live with an aunt, and my parents had to move to a family home out of town. But what really broke me at the time was the fact that it was one of my dad's siblings who had bought the house that rendered us homeless for a season.

And then my mum fell ill. For over a year, we had taken her to different hospitals and she had been misdiagnosed several times. Thankfully, one of my aunts paid for us to take her to a hospital with a higher medical standard. They did a scan and saw that she had a brain tumour.

I remember vividly the day the news came. I went into the bathroom and I cried and cried and cried. We had also been informed that we had to deposit thirty thousand pounds for her medical care in the UK. In the middle of our financial struggles, that was impossible. Thankfully, my dad's very supportive family members helped us and paid the bills on his behalf.

During that period, my relationship with my mum deepened. I would give her a bath, sleep with her in the hospital and go to work from the hospital. The experience also deepened my relationship with God.

One particular day, we were watching television and a preacher came on air. He said, "There is a woman watching with a brain tumour. You are healed."

I looked at my mum and told her that she was the one he was referring to. We both believed, and held on to that declaration.

The surgery was scheduled for the day after we arrived in the UK. I had never heard of or known anyone who had gone through a brain surgery and I was terrified; I thought anything that had to do with the brain was fatal. When the doctor began to tell us the probable side effects of the surgery, it got even scarier.

Thankfully, I wasn't alone. My younger brother was in London at the time and we were at the hospital with friends.

One of my friends taught us the song, "Because He lives, I can face tomorrow/ all fear is gone…"

It was the perfect song. It gave us hope. We kept singing it over and over again until she went in for the surgery.

It was the longest 5 hours of my life.

And then the doctor came out and said, "Your mum's case is phenomenal." Contrary to the norm, she was out of the anaesthesia immediately and the first word she said was, "Jesus".

# The Broken Little Girl

*"God doesn't reject broken vessels. He restores them and uses them for His glory"*
**–Omilola Oshikoya**

I once heard a story about a broken vessel.

The servants of a certain King used vessels to get water from the stream for the King's table. Among the vessels they used, one was broken. Each time they returned from the stream, the broken vessel got to the King's table empty. All the water had leaked out of it during the journey because of its cracks. This vessel began to feel very unworthy. It wanted to be like the other vessels who were perfect, the ones who got the opportunity to serve water to the King. If only it could be perfect like all the other vessels then life would be perfect and it would feel worthy. What this vessel didn't realise is that along the path from the stream to the Palace, beautiful flowers had begun to grow. It was such a beautiful sight to behold. The water that leaked from the broken vessel had watered the earth and caused the most beautiful flowers to grow, thereby beautifying the pathway to the palace.

This story moved me to tears.

If, like me, you can completely relate to the broken vessel, remember that there is a purpose for your brokenness. Embrace it; God will use it.

***

As a result of our financial difficulties, there was a lot of tension at home. My parents were always fighting and, apart from the words being thrown around, it was very violent, the kind of stuff you see in Hollywood movies.

Sometimes we were caught in the crossfire. Sometimes these fights were taken to the streets, and neighbours would come to try to stop the fights. Sometimes we would be woken up in the middle of the night. Sometimes I would hear people shouting and run out of my room, only to find out that nothing was happening. Sometimes my mum would be locked out of the house and we would beg my dad to let her in. Sometimes my dad would threaten to leave us to start another family. Once, my mum left for two weeks and I thought she wasn't coming back. The violence, infidelity and everything scared me to the core, and I used to wish my parents would get divorced so that we could have peace.

My dad's family members rarely came to visit and it made me feel insecure and unloved. At some point, we lived in the same building as one of my aunts, and I would watch as family members would visit her flat downstairs but never come up to visit us.

When I was around the age of five, the house help who had been with us practically since I was born used to touch me. He would use his fingers to play with the outer area of my private part, which would cause a sensation. I didn't even realise I had been abused until I watched an episode of the Oprah Winfrey show when I was around twelve.

As it turned out, the same house help who had abused me had returned to work for my parents. I avoided him until one day when he was rude to me. I lost it and reported the abuse to my parents.

My mum gave him the beating of his life and my dad sent him to the police station. I was so relieved; it felt like a burden had been lifted off me.

Then, one day, I heard my parents arguing about it.

The guilty house help had worked closely with my dad and, in the middle of all our troubles, the fact that he had been forced to lose a trusted helper became yet another source of frustration for him. And in his anger, I heard him tell my mum that it was our fault his help had been sacked.

I couldn't understand what I was hearing. His words took away the relief I'd felt after my abuser had been accosted, and I started to feel unloved and unworthy. It took me many years to understand that my dad hadn't meant to hurt me, took me years to understand that grownups say things in frustration that they don't mean. It was my dad who had sent him to the police station, after all; he had done that to protect me, because he loved me. But at that age I couldn't understand how he could blame me, and I became insecure.

Between this, the violent fights and my feelings of unworthiness, my relationship with my dad became strained. I vividly remember when I stopped running to jump on him whenever he came home from work. He had come home one day and we were in one of the living rooms. Normally, I would have run to greet him, but I just couldn't bring myself to.

Thankfully, our relationship is restored, to the glory of God. I know he loves me dearly and he would do anything to make me happy. He is a wonderful grandfather to my kids, and he spends a lot of time with them. He is also very supportive of me.

# The Lady and Her Quest For Love

I grew up to become a very insecure young lady. I was insecure about everything; I didn't like my friends visiting our home because we weren't rich, I was insecure about my looks and thought I was ugly, I didn't like the colour of my skin, I had a lot of pimples as an adolescent and, to top it all, the feeling of worthlessness from the abuse also remained. I spent most of my childhood wishing I could grow up quickly, so that I could get away from it all. I couldn't wait to get married so that I could leave the house and be with someone who loved me.

So when a boy who'd just joined the school in SS2 (year 11) asked me out, I said yes immediately, which was not cool. I was supposed to 'front' for some time but I didn't, I was so eager to have a boyfriend because most of my mates were dating already! This relationship led to my first kiss and only lasted about two weeks.

My second relationship was a lot better. He was sweet and treated me like a queen. He would write love letters and spray his perfume on it; he also made a mix-tape for me. I used to be so excited to go to school daily so I could see him! He was a real gentleman. He was a year ahead of me and so he took me to Prom, which was lucky for me because my year didn't get the chance to go to Prom.

The relationship ended after he left to go to school abroad. It was difficult to communicate then, without mobile phones, so it fizzled out.

At this point, my need for love and affirmation was so intense that I was willing to date or have a 'thing' with anyone who showed me any sort of interest; I was just so happy that someone could actually like me or find me attractive.

I got into my first proper relationship when I was 18. I met him at a party at my friend's house when I was 17, just after we had finished our final exams in secondary school. We started dating officially a year later, just before I went to University.

He was 6 years older than me and had had a difficult childhood. We would talk about our difficult experiences and we bonded that way. He had a great singing voice and he would always sing love songs to me. I was over the moon.

The relationship became quite intense because, at this point, most of my friends had gone to school abroad and he filled the vacuum. I thought he was my knight in shining armour.

The first time he said 'I love you', my world changed. Finally, I thought, I'd found someone who loved me. The love I had needed so desperately, I thought I'd found in this man, and I gave my virginity to him.

Everything was alright until I moved to England to study, leaving him in Nigeria – where he worked. He became very possessive. I would spend the time when I should have been sleeping, studying or hanging out with my friends, in front of a computer screen on MSN chat or sending emails back and forth. We would chat for hours. I couldn't do anything or go anywhere with my friends without his permission. My friends at University often wondered why I was restricted by someone who wasn't even in the country.

For example, once I was too scared to go on a trip to Scotland with my friends because I was scared of his reaction. I craved the attention and the affection but the distance made it hard to get either, and my insecurities resurfaced. In the process, I gave into someone else.

I had met this guy a long time ago and, as we say here, he was "on my case." He gave me the attention my insecure heart craved, and I cheated on my boyfriend.

It was a one-off and I told him about it, I promised it would never happen again. He was hurt, but we hung in there. I was relieved and grateful.

Eventually, he moved to the UK for his masters and it devolved into a very emotionally unhealthy relationship, but I didn't care. I mean, who else would love me with all my baggage? We were two broken people trying to find solace in each other, but we just ended up hurting each other; hurting ourselves.

I had grown up in the Catholic Church. My mother was a staunch Catholic and I used to follow her to 6:30am mass every morning. I found myself in a Pentecostal Church for the first time when my boyfriend took me. It was a completely different experience from what I had been accustomed to and I loved it. I started going to a Pentecostal church in University and I always looked forward to going to church.

I remember when I decided I wasn't going to be Catholic anymore. My mother had come to stay with me in school and, when I told her my decision, we had a huge fight. But I was bold in my decision to follow God's leading and, even in the middle of my mess, I fell in love with Jesus and began to just seek Him. I got baptised, joined the choir and prophetic dancing, and became very prayerful. I literally threw myself into seeking God.

At the same time as I was boldly seeking God for myself, I still lived a life of fun, clubbing and partying. I struggled with the two, and started to have two separate lives: I had my Church life and my Church friends, and I had my fun life and my other friends.

Also, at the same time as I was actively focusing on Jesus, I remained in the abusive relationship with the boyfriend who had introduced me to the church I now loved so much.

The relationship continued after I graduated from university. It continued even when he started dating someone else at the same time as he was dating me.

All along, I had thought they were just friends, and I found out that they were actually dating at a party. I accosted them at the party and he ended up hitting me that day.

It was chaotic. My friends were at the party and they couldn't believe it. They advised me to leave him. My childhood friends had always had reservations about this relationship, but the weirdest thing was that, instead of being upset at him, I was upset that everyone knew about it because I didn't want the relationship to end. However, he had done the 'unforgivable' in front of witnesses, and I was under pressure to break up with him. He apologised several times, even turning up at my doorstep at 4 am. But the relationship eventually ended, and I went to Nigeria for about three months.

My cousin's engagement ceremony happened to fall during my time in Lagos, where I spotted a handsome and mysterious man. He was dancing with the couple and there was someone with him so I thought he was taken, but he was so good-looking, I couldn't tear my eyes away. At the wedding, I was a bridesmaid and he was a groomsman.

At some point during the wedding reception I went out for some air, and to my surprise, this same man came to ask me my name.

Just a few months before the wedding, we were at my cousin's house in London. Her fiancé was in town, and we were just hanging out in the living room as a family.

I jokingly said to her fiancé, "Ah, do you have any fine, single, eligible friends?"

"There's one guy, o," he said, "He's a very good guy. A very principled, one-woman kind of guy." He said many nice things about him.

It turned out that this handsome man was the very same person my cousin's fiancé had talked about, and they hadn't even discussed it!

It was definitely meant to be.

After he asked for my name, he left. I noticed him staring at me a few times during the party but that was it.

It was Christmas in Lagos, which meant parties or clubbing every night of the week. I kept bumping into this mysterious man everywhere and, sometimes, he would even ask me to dance. I love to dance, he was a very good dancer, and we would dance for hours. He had already won my heart, but he hadn't even asked me for my number. That infuriated me, but I fought the urge to ask him for his and we went our separate ways.

In Lagos, once the Christmas holidays are over, everyone goes back to their routine. I had thought about moving back to the country, so I was in town for three months. Since we weren't bumping into each other anymore, the idea of Mr Mysterious had fizzled out. Plus, he had never asked for my number, and he never called.

I wasn't working and I was bored. I ended up talking to another guy I had fancied since I was in my teens; let's call him Mr Player. He didn't treat me right, he was only interested in being physical with me and, once he got what he wanted, the calls stopped. I got the message and a few weeks later, I decided I was moving back to the UK.

On the day I was going back to the UK, I got a call.

I was in the car doing last-minute activities ahead of my trip when my phone rang. I asked who was calling and thought it was Mr Player. I was surprised to find out it was actually Mr Mysterious!

I asked him why he hadn't asked for my number and why he hadn't called me all this while. He said he had been preparing for his law school finals and hadn't wanted any distractions. Apparently, he had also been praying to God to choose a wife for him – but I found out about this later. It was a quick call, and he only called twice while I was in England because he was still preparing for his final exams.

I moved back to England and stayed with my older brother's friend, and I spent my days looking for a job. I became lonely and needy again. I considered giving my ex another chance, but I found out that he was now fully seeing the woman he had cheated on me with.

My friends from University asked me to stay with them, which really helped with the loneliness. I found solace in church until one day when my ex came to church with the other girl. I couldn't believe it. I thought he did it to hurt me because she was Muslim and not even Christian.

That day, after the service, we all walked to the station together, him, her and me. I still don't know how I did it. It was humiliating.

My turning point came when I stumbled on my cousin's copy of, "The Lady, Her Lover and Her Lord" by TD Jakes. This book changed my life. In it, TD Jakes focuses on three crucial relationships in a woman's life: A relationship with herself, with her man and with God.[1]

For the first time, I heard about the concept of loving yourself, and I realised that I actually didn't love myself.

I had always been afraid of being alone, and I could never imagine taking myself out on a date, but I learnt it was okay to take myself out to dinner or to go to the cinema by myself. Before I read this book, I could never have imagined doing either.

I tried it. I went to Nandos myself. Initially it was uncomfortable, but something broke that day. I learnt that being alone does not mean being lonely. I learnt that your single years are actually some of your most precious times. I learnt that it was okay to be alone. I learnt to enjoy my own company and I began to fall in love with myself.

I came to realise that you attract who you are, and how you treat yourself determines how others will treat you. I also realized that all my relationships prior to this had been based on need and not love.

The book taught me about the kind of man I deserved; the kind of man God wanted me to be with. I began to understand who I was in Christ. I began to see my worth and value according to His word. I realized that I didn't need the love of any man, and that even though I was by myself, I wasn't alone. I had the author of Love with me and I was loved.

---

[1] "Without a doubt, we all want to experience love, but we must ask, Are we in love with others or are we in love with the idea of being in love? Many are the women, and men as well, who have turned to the arms of someone looking for the assurance that ultimately must come from within. ...Then and only then can we determine whether we are loving others because they are lovable or because we are so famished for love that we will settle for anyone or anything that gives to us what we should give to ourselves."

-TD Jakes, From *The Lady, Her Lover and Her Lord.*

I found love in Jesus, and this realization allowed me to move on from that relationship.

# The One

Not too long after, my friend's brother in law tried to hook me up with his friend. Let us call him Mr Potential. His girlfriend had just broken up with him and he was looking for a fresh start.

We got on quite well. For the first time, I was treated like a Queen. He wooed me. He took me out on really nice dates. He was a dedicated Christian who loved God. We talked about God a lot and we went to church together a few times, but he was really affected by his ex and wasn't completely over her. He had also been talking to another girl and trying to decide which one of us to choose. Once I found out, I got put off. He also raised his voice at me once and this was a cause for concern.

One day, Mr Mysterious called me again. We spoke for a long while and I was intrigued. He was unlike any other man I had met. True to his reputation, he really seemed to be a one-woman type of man. He had only been in two long-term relationships and he had never dated a Nigerian or black woman. He seemed to be a gentleman and was very principled, but he didn't call again –because of his exams.

At this point, Mr Potential was still wooing me, so when I received a huge bouquet of white roses on my birthday I immediately called Mr Potential to say thank you, but it turned out he hadn't sent them.

When Mr Mysterious called to ask if I got the flowers, I was over the moon. We talked for a little while and he said he was coming to London that summer.

I was excited to finally get to know him but, again, I was disappointed. He didn't come.

I moved back to Lagos that summer. Actually, the aunt who I had been staying with at the time insisted I move back and bought my ticket. My plan was to run back to London after a week! Alas, a week is now 13 years later.

Since I was in Lagos, and Mr Mysterious had finally finished his exams, he now had time for me. We spoke every day on the phone and he came to visit me every day.

We officially started dating ten months after we met. This was the first relationship I had entered into out of love and not out of need.

I remember our first date. I ordered a baguette, but when it came it was really hard and I made a mess of my food. I really wanted to impress this fine, phonetics-speaking man. Luckily, we had a good laugh about it.

He took me on romantic dates; we once spent a night at a beach house. We became the best of friends and we spent all our time together. I didn't have a car, and he would pick me up every morning, drop me at work before he went to work, and take me back home every day. We were very social, always going to parties, and we were the fashionable 'Posh and Becks' among our friends, after Victoria and David Beckham.

While we were dating, his mum had to travel abroad to help his sister who had just given birth to twins, leaving him at home to take care of his father.

I was in awe of the way he looked after his father. Aside from making sure he was okay, he would cook for him. When I say cook, I mean he would make the most complex meals and the food tasted delicious. That's when I knew He was The One. Even though I can cook, I don't like cooking, so this was an added bonus for me. Growing up, I had always admired the qualities of my friend's dad who was very hands on at home, and I'd hoped to marry someone like that.

He was also there for me when I went through some tough times. When we didn't have a home, he would come and spend time with me at my aunt's house, which was quite far from where he lived. I was separated from my family and was very lonely, and he was always there. When my mum was diagnosed with the tumour he would help me take care of her, and when we went to London for the surgery he would call us every day.

Not long after we returned to Lagos from the surgery, it was my 24th birthday. He took me out to dinner at a fancy restaurant and bought me really nice gifts. It was also one of our older friend's birthdays that day and he told me that we were going to her birthday party, but before that he took me out for drinks at Eko Hotel, where we had met.

When we got there we went for a romantic walk, and then he began to talk quite deeply. I can't remember exactly what he said because all of a sudden he got down on one knee and asked me to marry him. It was the exact same spot he had come to ask for my name on the first day we met.

I couldn't believe it. I fell on my knees and hugged him and said yes. I was over the moon. I was so excited and wanted to call my family and friends but he didn't let me, he said we were running late for the birthday party. We got there and it turned out to be a surprise party for me with all my loved ones. I burst into tears of joy and gratitude.

When the reality of the fact that I was actually getting married hit me, all the demons that had pursued me from my childhood hit me with full force.

I was very scared of marriage. Love wasn't enough anymore. I was 24 when he proposed, and I was the first of my friends to get married.

I was also worried that we didn't have the same ambitions. We had discussed our desires in life and they were quite different. I had a mission to be rich, and rich quick. My husband, on the other hand, was focused on his vision and he was content to follow it through, but I felt that he didn't have the same hunger or drive as I did. And in truth, he didn't – I was driven by fear and he was driven by Love, but I didn't realise it then. He had a plan for his career but it was not as aggressive as I wanted. I wanted us to be rich quickly.

I didn't realise that what I called 'drive' was my childhood fears in full force. I was afraid of facing financial difficulty again. I didn't want to go through the same challenges I went through as a child.

I was afraid to bring this up with him but I eventually did. We spoke about everything in great detail and he allayed my fears, but I underestimated how deep the demons had gone, and how much damage had been done.

Around this time, Mr Player came back calling. I guess he had thought I would always be there whenever he was ready to settle down, and the reality that I was engaged made him wake up. He had a hunger for money like I did, so I wondered if I was meant to be with him instead. I was confused; they even had the same name. Was I making a mistake? It felt like I had to choose between the two of them.

What I didn't realize was that it was a distraction, and that it was my fear that had created room for it. I remember telling my mum about my confusion and she wrote me a long letter that put everything in perspective. She said that God had blessed me with a good man who loved me and I wanted to throw it away. With regards to my fears about money, she said, "It is God who blesses, and He decides who He wants to bless."

Thank God for mothers with vision. I prayed and asked God for a sign to confirm His choice and, shortly after, my fiancé got this incredible, mind-blowing bonus at his old place of work. Like my mum had said, God chooses who he will bless. I took it as confirmation that as long as we had God, we would be fine.

Still, the night before our registry wedding, I wept in fear. But I knew it was God's plan. I did it very afraid, and Mr Mysterious became Mr Right.

***

There were two things I wanted in a man. First, I wanted a man who feared God, and secondly, I wanted a man who was my cheerleader. This was important to me because my dad didn't want my mum to work. My husband met both requirements, and it didn't hurt that he was also really good-looking. I couldn't have asked for more.

I had married the man of my dreams, but I still had a whole lot of baggage and didn't realise it.

Our marriage went through its usual challenges at the beginning; mostly personality clashes. I'm very carefree while my husband is very particular about the way he wants his things, but we eventually learnt to compromise.

We partied a lot during the earlier years and were always out socializing together, which we both loved, but the downside to this was that we didn't get to spend enough quality time alone. Still, things were pretty okay until I moved jobs, started working in investment banking and earning more money than my husband.

# My Career vs. My Marriage

One of my rich aunts worked in a bank and I wanted to follow in her footsteps, so I studied Finance and Accounting. I believed that all the problems my parents had had at home had been caused by a lack of money, so I was determined to be a Rich Woman with a nice sports car and a flat in a highbrow part of town.

When I moved back to Nigeria I worked in one of the top four accounting firms in the world for three years, but I soon got bored with accounting. Investment banking seemed more interesting to me; it had a huge pay package and was a faster way to achieve my dreams of being rich, so I changed careers.

I loved everything about investment banking. I loved the intellectual conversations with colleagues. I loved working on dynamic and interesting transactions, which we used to call 'sexy' transactions. I loved structuring an infrastructure fund, a private jet business, a luxury hotel on a golf course, agriculture & health care funds, an urban parking system under a private-public partnership, a mixed use retail complex which consisted of a world class shopping mall, hotel and hotel apartments overlooking a golf course... I loved the negotiations. I loved hosting board meetings. I loved networking and the opportunities to meet dignitaries such as the Executive Governor of Lagos State and the Director General of the Stock Exchange. I loved travelling to different countries. I loved the trendy, high fashion suits; I would even wear a tie to work. I didn't quite like the number crunching but I always found my way around it.

I loved my new career. I had very big dreams. I was going to become Minister of Finance or manage an infrastructure fund. I ended up working in one of the best non-bank financial institutions in Nigeria and was promoted to middle management. I loved my job. I loved the company and I was earning a good salary. I was also very ambitious and so I always had a side hustle that sometimes brought me more income than my regular salary. I would sell tunics, underwear or supply corporate gifts. The senior management liked me and had big plans for me.

After a few years, the excitement of the new job fizzled out. I would leave the house at 5 or 6 in the morning to get to work before 7.30am, and I would get home on average around 8 pm and sometimes later. I never saw my kids in the morning and, by the time I got home at night, they'd be asleep. I couldn't do the school runs because I had to leave the house very early to beat traffic, since our home was not near my work place. My husband, on the other hand, didn't have to leave so early, and his office was closer to the house.

I had two nannies to take care of my children but there was no nanny-equivalent to fill in my role as a mother and wife, and my marriage suffered. A family member once advised me to get a job that closed earlier, and this made me very angry.

I also wasn't watching the correlation between how much I was earning and how much I was spending. I earned a lot, but I was spending more than I earned and was practically living from pay check to pay check. I was spending frivolously on hair, clothes and travel, with no clear financial plan. I had also taken on a debt that was highly unnecessary and the cost of repaying it was a burden.

At this point, my husband had changed jobs and started working for his father's company with his siblings. The fact that he worked for his dad brought back intensely fearful memories of my childhood. What if something happened? What if we lost everything? What if we had to go through the same challenges I'd faced as a child? Even as it was, I felt we were barely making ends meet.

Fear is real. It prevents you from thinking logically. It prevents you from seeing beyond your current situation. It is like putting an opaque object in front of your lens and all you can see is darkness. It is truly the acronym for False Evidence Appearing Real.

Work stopped being fulfilling. At this point we had started developing complex financial models and I detested it. I knew this wasn't what I wanted to do anymore and I wanted to find my passion. I wanted to discover my gifts and talents and walk in purpose and I was so tired of chasing money but by this time, because of my new job, I earned more money than my husband and the thought of being solely dependent on him was more than I could bear, particularly since he worked in his father's company like my father. We definitely couldn't survive on his income alone, I thought, so I couldn't even consider quitting my job.

I was trapped, a slave to my fear of poverty.

I had put unnecessary stress on myself in my quest for the pursuit of money and I transferred this burden to my husband. Even though it was unfair of me to judge him based on my past, I was very critical. Sometimes, when we had arguments, I said a lot of things that a woman shouldn't say to a man, especially not to her husband, and this strained our relationship. A woman should always build her man up, but I spent all my energy tearing him down. I would compare him to other people, use adjectives that were demeaning, blame him for my misery. I didn't believe in him or his vision. I wanted him to have the same kind of vision I wanted. I wanted him to be hungry for money. I wanted him to leave his father's firm and start his own company. It seemed like everyone was prospering financially around us except for us.

We stopped talking as much, stopped sharing each other's concerns or burdens like we should have. We became distant. We wouldn't talk for days. We lived in the same house but lived separate lives. I felt very alone and I'm sure he must have felt the same way. I began to resent him and question if I'd really heard from God about marrying him. I would cry every day, on the way home from work and even at home.

# Tests and Trials

At this point I felt it was only God who could save me and my marriage, so I started to pray. I decided to fast and pray once a week for my husband to seek God more, and for God to bless us. I started fasting with two other ladies who also wanted to leave their jobs. Shortly after we started fasting, both of the ladies got their breakthroughs. My situation was still the same.

A few weeks after I started fasting for my husband, the greatest test of our marriage began.

I was on a flight back from my first international trip for the company. I had recently started working on a new project at work and it involved a lot of travelling. I was excited to represent my organisation internationally at this conference. I had always dreamed of travelling for work, so when the opportunity came I jumped at it. It was a conference at a really nice resort and I thoroughly enjoyed the trip.

On my way back, I didn't like the seat I had been given on the plane because it was near the toilet. The flight was not full and so there were a few empty seats. I waited till I was sure most people had boarded the flight and, when it was close to take off time, I saw two empty seats and quickly moved. Not too long after, a man came to sit next to me. Let's call him Mr Temptation. I got up to move but he said it was fine. He was dressed really well and was good looking.

We didn't talk much, initially. I had been fasting and I broke my fast on the plane, then we started talking.

He asked my name and told me his. I knew someone with the same surname and she happened to be his cousin. He was married with kids, and we had a great conversation about work and about our families. We got on really well and chatted most of the flight. He gave me some ideas on one of the projects I was working on and promised to follow up. He even mentioned that he wanted to meet my husband, and we exchanged business cards. I even told my husband about him when I got home that evening.

Then, for some reason, I kept thinking about him. I sent him an email following up on our work discussions but, truthfully, I was intrigued. We started chatting via blackberry messenger and then once in a while on the phone.

What I didn't realize was that some seeds had been sown. At this point, my husband and I would go through long periods of not talking and this man filled the vacuum. What was really weird was that, for some odd reason, someone I had never seen before in my entire life suddenly began to appear wherever I went. We would chat about random things and before you know it, we started flirting.

Soon, I began to realize that it was becoming more than a platonic work relationship and I decided to cut off all communication with him.

This was the first of many failed attempts.

We started talking again a few months later. It was my very good friend's birthday and she was having a party. I went there early to help her get ready, and she started talking about some good-looking friend of hers who was coming from London for her birthday. It turned out to be Mr Temptation.

It was stolen moments. We would chat while I was at work. We would chat on the way home. He lived abroad, in a different country from his wife and kids, and he travelled quite a bit, so he had a lot of time to chat. I'm a talker, and he made time to talk with me.

He told me he had three girlfriends in different countries. He said he had recently broken up with them and was looking for one girlfriend he could focus on. A married woman would be his preferred choice now because she wouldn't be high maintenance, emotionally. I had never heard anything like this in my entire life and his honesty fascinated me. When we started talking, his marriage was about to hit the ten-year mark. He said the first time he cheated on his wife was when they were about to hit the five-year mark. He said the fifth year of marriage is a very crucial year.

Coincidentally, I was about to mark my fifth anniversary as well.

We spoke about God. He used to be a devoted Christian, a tongue-speaking, Pastor's boy, but something happened along the way. I asked him what changed but he never said, I could sense that Christianity was now just a religion for him.

I asked him if he ever felt guilty about his affairs and he said he knew how he did penance for whatever he did wrong.

He had come from humble beginnings and worked his way up, and he was enjoying his success, new social life and circle.

It was really hard to put an end to it. I would randomly spot him driving on the road or see him in unexpected places. There were moments when I would say, "I can't do this; even if it is not for my husband's sake, then for God's sake," and I would cut him off. After a few months we would start chatting again, one of us would give in and call the other and it would become more intense, and he would say it wasn't fair for me to have cut him off.

At some point I convinced myself that I wasn't doing anything bad since it wasn't physical; we were only chatting, after all. From our conversations, I believe he was attracted to the fact that I was young, intelligent, independent, ambitious, and successful, and from a certain social circle that he now had the privilege of being a part of because of his wealth. He liked the new life he was living. He had grown up a little overweight and had only recently lost weight, so he had a new confidence with his new body.

Towards my fifth wedding anniversary I cut him off again and decided to work on my marriage. My husband had a wonderful surprise party for me to mark my birthday – which is a day after my anniversary – and he also took me on a really romantic holiday out of town.

Then when I got back to work, I received a surprise package. It was a birthday present from Mr Temptation, a wristwatch he had probably bought on one of his airport trips. I wasn't impressed. I gave it out.

Once, after I had cut off communication again for a few months, I noticed that someone had put his picture up as her display picture, wishing him a happy birthday. The really strange thing about that was that it was also my husband's birthday! I couldn't believe it. How in the world could it be that my husband and this man shared the same birthday? I began to think that there was more to this than meets the ordinary eye.

I called him and told him I couldn't believe he had the same birthday as my husband and we started chatting yet again. It seemed like all my attempts to cut him off proved abortive.

Early the following year, my friend's brother passed away at the age of 31. He was such a good-looking man with a lot of potential. He had a really good job and was making good money but he died suddenly.

His death really shook me and, on top of that, my mum had just been diagnosed with a brain tumour for the second time. At this point I wasn't chatting with Mr Temptation anymore. I travelled with my mum to the UK for 6 weeks and I had a lot of time to reflect.

Then the Dana Crash happened.

I had started chatting with Mr Temptation yet again when I went on another work trip to Dubai. I was bored and reached out. This season became quite intense because we had gone a few months without chatting, and we had been chatting when news of the crash came out. Maybe if this crash hadn't happened I would have given into temptation fully.

I knew a couple of people on the plane and I was devastated. I began to think deeply about my life. Many of the people who died had been young people with their lives ahead of them.

I began to wonder, surely there must be more to life than to chase money. There must be more to life than waking up early to go to a job that I didn't like. What if I died? Had I fulfilled my purpose? How did I spend my time? Did I spend it with my loved ones? The reality of the sin and lie I was living was also quite glaring. Would God approve of my actions over the last couple of years with this strange man?

I realised I wanted to leave my job but I couldn't, however I decided to be real with my husband, to tell him about my struggles and my temptations and to give our marriage a chance. But how was I going to tell him?

It all came out the day before my birthday. We were at the boat club and I asked to use my husband's phone. He was a bit evasive and I became suspicious. I decided to go through his BBM timeline and I saw the names of two random girls. I checked the chats and they were completely innocent but I flipped and decided to make a big deal out of it and make him feel guilty when we got home. I was using reverse psychology. I was obviously looking for how to flip this on him. I wanted to hurt him and I didn't even know why. So I blurted it out and said, "Well, there's a guy I have been chatting with...." I ended up telling him everything.

He couldn't believe it. He asked me if we had been physical and I said no. He didn't sleep in the room that night.

The next time Mr Temptation called, I told him that I had told my husband and that he shouldn't call me anymore. This was the end of a two-year struggle, or so I thought.

The day after I told my husband, he got into a serious car accident on his way home. A few months later, after we had a random fight, he got into another accident and his car flipped on the bridge. The car was a complete write-off, and it was only by God's grace that he came out of it unscathed.

Around this time there was a lot of pressure at work. My boss had been dropping the ball and he was being investigated for fraudulent activities. As the most experienced member of the team, a lot of the work fell to me. I desperately wanted to leave, but I couldn't.

It didn't help that I was surrounded by friends who were entrepreneurs. I secretly envied the fact that they were in charge of their own time. We would all hang out on Sunday and I hated the fact that I was the only one who had to wake up early the next day for work. I would regularly pass comments about hating my job but I never actually mentioned to my husband that I wanted to leave. Perhaps I already assumed it was pointless because I was too scared to leave, anyway.

I began to resent my husband.

What I didn't realize was it had absolutely nothing to do with him. I was the one who chose to pursue a career that didn't give me fulfilment, because of my childhood fears and insecurities.

I remember a conversation with one of my aunts when I was younger. She had just told one of her daughters to marry to a rich man. But I had dreams to be rich on my own, so I told her that all I wanted was a man who supported my ambitions. I had prayed for exactly that, a man who would be my greatest cheerleader, and God had answered my prayers. My husband is the most supportive man, and he has been since we were dating. Once, when he was still doing his youth service, I had registered to do my ACCA exams and he paid for it. It cost 500 pounds, which was a lot of money at the time, especially for a Youth Corper. He is also very supportive with regard to the children; he's always there when I can't be. He's an amazing father.

I had exactly what I wanted but it suddenly wasn't enough. I was unfulfilled, I was unhappy, and my marriage was on the brink of collapse. I eventually began to seek God again, because I realised that He was the only One who could help me.

I joined a discipleship class called MasterLife at my church, Guiding Light Assembly, and it helped me grow closer to God. It was a small group and we grew close as we supported one another on our journeys. One day I opened up to the group, I shared how unfulfilled I was, and they began to pray for me.

Things started to change drastically once they began to pray for, and with, me.

During one of our weekly Wednesday meetings, my discipleship group suggested that I take some time out, maybe travel away with my husband, to discuss things.

The Saturday after, my husband had a freak accident and broke his entire patella tendon in his knee. He had to have surgery and we decided it was best to travel abroad for it so, on Sunday, we went to my office to send an email to my mum's doctor, to get recommendations for a surgeon for my husband.

As we got into the office, we bumped into the Head of Human Resources. We were quite close and she wanted to speak to me about something important. She said we should chat on Monday, but I decided to go see her immediately.

She began to tell me the great plans management had for me. My boss had been laid off and I was expected to take up his responsibilities. Senior management was entrusting me with this huge responsibility and it was the opportunity of a lifetime.

"Management is looking up to you," she said, "I told them you can handle it. You'll need to put things in place for your family so you can focus on work. This is a good opportunity for you."

Basically, it was my time to 'shine'.

My life was flashing before me during our conversation. It felt like she had asked me to choose between my career and my family, between my career and my life.

To some other people, this would be the greatest news ever, but for me she was saying the exact opposite of what I wanted to hear. I was already not spending enough time with my children. I already had two nannies. What else did I need to put in place for my family?

I said thank you and left her office. It felt like I was at a crossroad and I had to choose between two paths. One path would lead to a successful career and money and the other path would lead to my family. I shut down my computer and my husband and I left the office.

I was driving because my husband was in a cast, and he was in the back seat, and by the time we got on the street I broke down crying uncontrollably. I had had enough. I couldn't take it anymore. Here I was going abroad again for 2 weeks on another medical trip in the same year I had travelled to the UK for six weeks with my mum for the brain surgery. I was confused, exhausted and fed-up.

Then for the first time, my husband said, "It's okay, Omi, you can resign."

# Doing it Afraid

My husband's surgery was very successful, to the glory of God. We were required to stay in London for two weeks while he recovered and, since he was not physically mobile, and it was winter, we were stuck in the flat for most of the time.

I had a lot of time to reflect. I still couldn't believe my husband had given me permission to quit my job. I hadn't quite been able to process it because the surgery had taken up all my attention, but now there was nothing to do but think.

Again, I went back to God.

Now, my husband's consent was very important to me. As his wife, I am under his authority, and God expects me to submit to him. I knew God wanted me to leave my job but I told Him that I couldn't make a major decision that would affect our entire family without my husband's assent. I was honest with God about that.

So God stepped in. He touched my husband's heart and I now had the go-ahead I'd been seeking.

Now that I had his permission, I realized that all the reasons I had given myself for not quitting earlier had been excuses. The truth is that, as unhappy as I was, my fear of poverty was still greater than my fear of living a life without purpose. I had held on to my husband's consent as the final excuse, and now that he had freely given it, I had to come face to face with the decision before me.

What was I supposed to do when I resigned? It wasn't like I had a business opportunity that I was going to focus on. Yes, I had side hustles, but none of them were viable business ventures; I couldn't leave investment banking to sell tunics! I had no Plan B, and surely God wasn't going to tell me to resign without a Plan B.

One of those days, when I was having my quiet time with God, He led me to the book of Genesis chapter twelve when He told Abraham to leave the land that he was in:

> *Now the Lord said to Abram, "Go from your country and your kindred and your father's house to the land that I will show you...."*
> **Genesis 12:1 (ESV)**

Wow, that was very profound for me. You mean it was possible for God to ask you to go somewhere without showing you where?

As if that wasn't enough, God gave me another confirmation. My Bible at the time was a Joyce Meyer Bible. On the page after the passage, she had a narrative where she talked about how God leads you one step at a time.[2] That was all the confirmation I needed and I knew God was speaking to me.

I decided to resign.

As soon as we got back to Lagos, I walked up to the Executive Director's office and told him I was resigning. It was

---

[2] "When God gave Abraham this instruction, He gave him only one step, not step two. Abraham would not get to step two until he had accomplished step one. This is so simple, but so profound. God gives us direction one step at a time."

– From the *Joyce Meyer Bible*

the hardest thing for me to do. I broke down crying when I was telling him and he really couldn't understand it. If I didn't want to resign then why was I doing so?

He told me that I'd had a rough year and maybe I just needed some time off. He said they would give me extra time off to rest. This is me, who had already taken 8 weeks off on medical leave and another 2 weeks on vacation in one year – a total of 10 weeks – even though I was only entitled to 5, and he was still willing to give me more time off. He didn't want me to resign, and neither did the other senior management staff of the company.

But the thing is that I had heard from God and had no choice but to obey.

Was it scary? Absolutely. I was petrified. People thought I was crazy.

Someone I really looked up to said to me, "Omi, it is okay to fail."

She thought I had failed.

I remember going to see a family member and she said, "Hello, the jobless girl is here."

It was definitely one of the scariest times of my life but because I had God and the approval of my husband, I was fine. I also had my family, my parents and siblings, my prayer partner, my discipleship group members, my cousin and one or two colleagues who encouraged me to do it afraid. I did it very afraid.

Did I make a mistake? Did I fail? Was this the best decision of my life?

For one, I wouldn't be writing this book if I didn't do it afraid. God has opened unimaginable doors for me in the last four years since I resigned from my job, none of which would have happened if I wasn't obedient to God's call on my life.

Now I'm living a purpose-filled and purpose-driven life.

So many people have been impacted by the 'Do it Afraid' mantra. Would this have been possible if I hadn't been obedient? Possibly, because God's work will always be carried out. If I had been disobedient He would have found someone else to work through, even if He had to turn stones to human beings to do His work, and I'm so thankful to Him for giving me the grace to be obedient.

# Falling Into Temptation

*"When you are tempted, He will also provide a way out so that you can endure it."*
**1 Corinthians 10:13 (NIV)**

After I resigned, I began to wait on God to show me what I was supposed to do next. At the beginning, one or two consulting jobs came up. In fact at some point I got a very lucrative job offer to work for just two days a week and the pay was very attractive. I didn't see anything wrong with it.

Then I was doing my quiet time that day and I read **1 Samuel Chapter 15:**

> *'Samuel said to Saul, "...Thus says the Lord of hosts, 'I have noted what Amalek did to Israel in opposing them on the way when they came up out of Egypt. Now go and strike Amalek and devote to destruction all that they have. Do not spare them, but kill both man and woman, child and infant, ox and sheep, camel and donkey.'" And Saul defeated the Amalekites from Havilah as far as Shur, ... but Saul and the people spared Agag and the best of the sheep and of the oxen and of the fattened calves and the lambs, and all that was good, and would not utterly destroy them.*

*And Samuel said..."The Lord anointed you king over Israel. And the Lord sent you on a mission and said, 'Go, devote to destruction the sinners, the Amalekites, and fight against them until they are consumed.' Why then did you not obey the voice of the Lord? Why did you pounce on the spoil and do what was evil in the sight of the Lord?*

*Behold, to obey is better than sacrifice... The Lord has rejected you from being king over Israel."*

**1 Samuel 15: 1-3; 7-9; 17-19; 22-23; 26 (ESV)**

God had told King Saul to attack Amalek and destroy all that they had without sparing anyone. King Saul didn't do as God instructed but instead spared the King of the Amalekites and their best sheep, oxen, lambs, and other things. He claimed he had kept the produce to sacrifice to God, but because of this he was rejected as King and lost His anointing as God's chosen one.

On the next page in my bible, Joyce Meyer had a narrative about how, after she had resigned from her job based on instructions from God, she'd taken on a part-time role and ended up being fired from that role.[3]

---

[3] "When the Lord called me into the ministry, He asked me to quit my job, trust Him to provide what we needed above my husband's salary, and spend my time preparing for my future teaching ministry. I struggled tremendously with the thought of not working, and frankly, I was frightened by it. I had been working since I was thirteen years old and was accustomed to taking care of myself. Out of my fear, I decided to quit my full time job and get a part-time job instead of stopping work altogether as God had asked me to do. I had that job for only a short while before I was fired. I was normally a good employee and not the type who would be fired. Actually, the reason for my being fired was not related to my work; the office manager did not like me personally. I had disobeyed God, and he

God's message was clear, "Obedience is better than sacrifice."

I decided that it was in my best interest to be completely obedient. It was a tough decision because I remember writing in my journal that I only had about ₦524 left in my account, but I was going to trust God and turn down the job offer.

I became somewhat depressed afterwards. I had no job, no money, no direction or inclination to what I was supposed to be doing, and all these fears.

Don't get me wrong, God met all my needs, but I wasn't used to depending on God. I was used to depending on myself.

There was a lot of pressure on my husband and, around this time, I was also going through some fertility challenges. It was all too much, and it affected our relationship.

I remember seeing an international call on my phone, one day. I picked up and it was the same man I had been fighting temptation with. This was a year after we had stopped talking.

He told me he had a new job and had moved to a different country. He said he missed me. I told him a lot had happened and we couldn't talk anymore. I asked him to please not call me again.

The phone call caught me unawares and brought back memories, but I couldn't go down that route anymore. Everything had changed; my husband and I had been through so much. We were working on our marriage and I was determined to keep my focus squarely on what God had called me to.

---

withheld His favour in that job situation. I had tried to partially obey God and still needed to learn that obedience is not true obedience unless it is complete."

– From the *Joyce Meyer Bible*

That summer, I was very depressed. I wasn't doing anything with my time. The kids were home and I couldn't afford to take them on treats. We also couldn't afford to go away on holiday.

My good friend's sister was getting married; it just so happened that it was the same friend who was friends with Mr Temptation. She insisted that I couldn't miss the wedding; she even said she would pay for me to go with her. I really wanted to travel with my children but I knew we couldn't afford it, and this seemed to be a great opportunity for me. I needed the break. It had been an emotionally draining few months. I spoke to my husband about it and he said it was fine. I could go.

It was after this that she told me she had also invited Mr Temptation. She wasn't sure if he was going to come, and I didn't think he would travel to another continent just for a wedding. To keep me accountable, I had been open about my struggles to two of my friends, including this friend. I was worried about potentially seeing him in a foreign country, but I figured that if I had fought temptation for so long, I could fight it again. I prayed about it but I didn't tell my husband, because I didn't want him to worry. I also didn't want him to think I'd planned it.

When we arrived at our destination, my friend told me Mr. Temptation had confirmed that he would be there.

We were in the car driving when he called to tell her. After she told me he was coming, she said, "It is not fair that you cut him off abruptly. He really liked you and was even considering leaving his family for you. I think you should speak to him and explain things to him. He is not a bad person."

I pondered on what she said. I was petrified. The fear was real but I thought I could handle it. I sent a message to my best friend who was in the same country but in a different state. I also sent a message to my prayer partner to keep me accountable and to pray for me. With the benefit of hindsight, I should have called my husband and told him what was going on, but I was afraid.

All my demons followed me on this trip. From my fear of poverty to my fear of temptation, there was no escape. I had travelled to another country with my friend and all I took with me was $150. I could only eat when she was eating, and I had to follow her around as she shopped. I watched her buy things I couldn't afford and I felt like she wanted me to ask her for things, but I grew up with a fear of rejection and would rather die than ask anyone for anything. Now I know what I had was pride.

It was a very humbling experience. Add to that, the fact that my friend and I had a massive fight on the day of the pre-wedding party, and I was an emotional wreck. I was weak, I was furious and I wanted to go back to Nigeria.

I saw Mr Temptation at the party.

As soon as I walked in, my friend walked up to me and apologized for the fight we'd had. Then she said, "Guess who's here?"

I couldn't process the information. I couldn't believe I was in the same place as the man I'd fought temptation over for three years. I was afraid, so I walked to the other side of the party and stayed there the entire night. At the end of the night, when we went to the foyer to wait for cabs, he came to say hello but I ignored him.

On the morning of the wedding when I woke up, I couldn't have quiet time with God so I said a prayer to God to help me. Surprisingly, He called my room to ask for my friend. I recognized his voice but I pretended not to know who it was.

The odd thing was that my friend had been staying in the room next to mine when we had first arrived, so why was he calling my room to speak to her? She had also moved to another hotel closer to town where her family was staying and I told him she wasn't there, but I was surprised and even more nervous to find out he was staying at the same hotel as me.

I saw him at the wedding and he ignored me completely. The coin had flipped; I hadn't expected him to do that. I had prepared my defense if he came to talk to me but I hadn't prepared for him to blank me. Was it a strategy or had he moved on?

For some reason, I couldn't fight the urge to say hello. He was with someone when I walked up to him. I mentioned my surprise that we were staying in the same hotel and he said he had moved to a hotel closer to town. We didn't speak again.

The next day, I couldn't fight the urge to call him. My friend had booked my flight two days after she was leaving, which was later than most of the other guests. She'd said it was the only available flight she could find for me, so I was on my own for a few days. Coincidentally, he was also leaving on the same day as I was.

I found the number of his hotel online and told him we needed to talk.

We had planned to meet at a restaurant, but because there were so many Nigerians in town he asked me to come over to his hotel room instead. I decided to go. It had been a three-year battle and I told myself I needed the closure after everything.

The Word of God is true when it says that God always makes a way of escape in the face of temptation, but the question is whether or not we choose to take the way out. Just as I'd made the decision to go to his hotel, my husband sent me this really cute picture of our girls. I cried and cried as I looked at it, but I still chose to go.

I felt like I needed to just talk, talk about everything. We hadn't communicated for over a year but here we were in the same country again without it being planned. Was this the way my life was supposed to be? Was I fighting a battle I couldn't win?

I walked into his very fancy room at one of the most upmarket hotels in the city. I looked around. I saw a lady's handbag and what looked like an overnight bag in one of the wardrobes.

I teased him about the bag and he told me the most bizarre story. He said someone had left it in a cab they'd shared and he hadn't known what to do with it, so he took it, hoping to return it. I laughed and sat down.

He sat next to me and I just looked at him, a little perplexed at how I ended up here, right here in front of this man. He came closer and then I started crying. As I cried, he hugged me.

And then he kissed me.

*He kissed me?*

I was in shock. No way. We had finally become physical. But what was I expecting, since I'd gone all the way to his hotel willingly and in a sexy white maxi dress?

Up until then, I had consoled myself that as long as we weren't physical I hadn't committed adultery, but that was a lie. The bible says, *"But I tell you that anyone who looks at a woman lustfully has already committed adultery with her in his heart"* (**Matthew 5:28 NIV**).

I had already committed adultery from that first conversation on the plane. I had been attracted to him from that first day.

At that point, the guilt consumed me and I started crying even more. I had committed the ultimate sin; I had cheated on my husband. The kiss was as bad as the intent behind it and I had wilfully participated.

In my broken state, I told him I had to leave. He called a cab and I left.

Later, he called to check up on me, to make sure I was okay. He had gone clubbing and he came by at about 5 in the morning to check up on me for a few minutes. He said he would check out of his hotel and book a room in my hotel, so he could leave for the airport from there. Just to make sure I was alright.

With the benefit of hindsight, God provided another means of escape in the face of temptation. My best friend's sister was in town and she had asked me to go on a boat ride with her, but I felt so bad about what had happened and I didn't want to risk missing my flight, so I didn't go.

Later that day he booked another room and I went to see him. I didn't fight it. I was so tired of struggling to resist temptation. I had fought this for over three years and maybe this is how it was supposed to end, I was ready to let go. I let myself think, *maybe it's part of God's plan...* as he started to kiss me and take my clothes off.

But then something happened. I don't know what it was. Maybe it was because I had thought about God, maybe God was showing me that it was definitely *not* His plan, maybe it was because of the prayer I had prayed on the morning of the wedding but I suddenly said, "No, I can't do this."

I was at my most vulnerable. He could have urged me to go on, he could have even forced or raped me and it would have been seen as my fault, but he didn't. He didn't even try to convince me to go ahead, he respected my decision.

He simply said, "Now I know I respect you more than I want you."

From someone who had desired me for three years and finally had his chance, I was completely shocked. We were in a faraway country, we were alone, and there was nothing to stop us from going through with it. Absolutely nothing. But he stopped.

This is why I know the Grace of God.

> *"If I ascend into heaven, You are there; If I make my bed in hell, behold You are there.*
> **Psalm 139:8 NKJV**

God was there with me. He prevented me from sleeping with someone other than my husband and protected me from the consequences that would follow.

When you have sex with someone, you enter into a covenant with that person. When you sleep with someone other than your spouse, there are spiritual consequences.

Later, when I told a leader of my church about it, he showed me a verse that sort of explained what happened:

> *Then God said to him in the dream, "Yes, I know that you have done this in the integrity of your heart, and it was I who kept you from sinning against me. Therefore I did not let you touch her.*
>
> *Now then, return the man's wife... and you shall live. But if you do not return her, know that you shall surely die, you and all who are yours."*
> **Genesis 20:6-7 ESV**

In this passage, Abraham had lied to Abimelech. He had said Sarah was his sister out of his own selfish need to protect himself. Abraham had done the wrong thing, and yet God kept Sarah.

Just the same way, I had done the wrong thing, and yet God kept me from the consequences. What a merciful Father.

# Beauty For Ashes

Oh, I cried.

When I got back to Lagos I was petrified.

I have a close relationship with God and I knew that I couldn't get away with this; I knew God would require that I tell my husband even if I thought it was just a kiss.

I was shattered; I had betrayed God and my husband.

I shared this with my prayer partner. She cried because she knew the struggle I had gone through; we had prayed together for the last year and just like that I had given in. She asked me if it was only a kiss or there was more to this and I told her it was only a kiss.

It felt like my life was over. I didn't have a job, didn't even know what I was supposed to be doing with my life, had no money and now I was about to lose my marriage. I told her I had to tell my husband. She was afraid and said I shouldn't.

We prayed and she advised me to tell my Pastor what happened, and to ask for his advice. I also prayed and felt that was what I needed to do. My husband and I had gone to see my pastor for counseling in the past, so he had a bit of background information.

Around that same time it was my husband's birthday. To my surprise he wanted us to spend his birthday at night vigil.

The vigil was very prophetic. The Pastor preached on **Genesis Chapter 2:**

> *And the Lord God caused a deep sleep to fall on Adam, and he slept; and He took one of his ribs, and closed up the flesh in its place. Then the rib which the Lord God had taken from man He made into a woman, and He brought her to the man. And Adam said: "This is now bone of my bones, And flesh of my flesh; She shall be called Woman, Because she was taken out of Man." Therefore a man shall leave his father and mother and be joined to his wife, and they shall become one flesh. And they were both naked, the man and his wife, and were not ashamed.*
>
> **Genesis 2:21- 25 NKJV**

This was the first marriage.

The Pastor pointed out that, as soon as the first marriage was consummated, the devil came as their first visitor:

> *"Now the serpent was more cunning than any beast of the field which the Lord God had made. And he said to the woman, "Has God indeed said, 'You shall not eat of every tree of the garden'?" And the woman said to the serpent, "We may eat the fruit of the trees of the garden; but of the fruit of the tree which is in the midst of the garden, God has said, 'You shall not eat it, nor shall you touch it, lest you die.'"*
>
> **Genesis 3:2 NKJV**

He pointed out that satan is aware that a woman is a good thing, and so he attacks the woman.

> *He who finds a wife finds a good thing, And obtains favour from the Lord."*
> **Proverbs 18:22 NKJV**

He said a woman does her husband good, all the days of her life.

> *She does him good and not harm, all the days of her life."*
> **Proverbs 31:12 ESV**

He asked all the women to declare that from that day they would become 'Mrs Good'. He then asked the husbands to pray for their wives and declare that they are good. My husband laid his hands on me and began to pray for me. I felt like God was showing me mercy.

A few days later, I met with my pastor and told him what had happened. I broke down as I told him and narrated the entire episode between tears.

He was calm as I told him everything. He asked if I'd slept with him. I said no, and he comforted me with his words.

"Temptation is not sin," he said, and he told me God had forgiven me.

I told him I was going to tell my husband.

"I need to tell him, Pastor," I said.

Maybe I could tell him in front of my Pastor, I thought.

But he didn't think it was the best time to do so.

"He may not be able to handle it," he said, "give it some time. There will come a time when you can tell him."

He assured me of God's redeeming love and forgiveness. I felt much better and didn't feel condemned.

As I was leaving, he said, "Since you have free time, why don't you volunteer at the church office?"

That is how my 3-year journey working in Guiding Light Assembly started.

There was a vacancy in the publications department and I was required to write the weekly bulletin. Subsequently, my Pastor also wanted the church to open social media accounts.

Volunteering two days a week became more than 4 days a week, and I discovered my gifts and life's calling in Guiding Light Assembly. I set up the social media accounts and also joined the Heart of the Matter, a talk show that airs in 44 African countries and the UK.

Prior to this, I had no idea that I was supposed to work in media; finance was all I knew, but God had other plans.

Coincidentally, months before that, I went to an event and got talking with a US diplomat. We were introduced and we got talking. I told her I had recently left investment banking to follow purpose but I wasn't sure what I was supposed to be doing. She said, "I have a gift in helping people discover their purpose, you should be in Media."

Surely she must be joking, I thought, and that was the first and last time I thought about it. But all of a sudden, here I was.

My pain led me to discover my purpose. I had thought my life was ending but it was just starting.

Perhaps if that incident hadn't happened, I wouldn't have gone to see my Pastor and he wouldn't have asked me to volunteer at the church office. I began to work in a job that I loved. I began to earn money and doors began to open for me in the world of personal finance, life coaching and motivational speaking. I was hosting huge events and impacting lives. I became Africa's Premier Wealth Coach and the Do It Afraid queen.

I had time for my children and my marriage began to be restored.

It was in that place of purpose that I discovered, through my fertility issues, that I didn't have polycystic ovaries but rather I had pre-cancer cells. This discovery led to the successful removal of the pre-cancer cells, to the glory of God.

It was in that place of purpose that God blessed my husband and I with a beautiful baby boy. We conceived him three months after the pre-cancer cells were removed.

It was totally unplanned and an answer to prayer, even the delay in conceiving had been intentional by God. If I had gotten pregnant when I wanted to, it would have aggravated the pre-cancer cells.

> "And we know that ALL things work together for good to those who love God, to those who are called according to His purpose.
> **Romans 8:28 NKJV**

Things had worked for my good, but what about my husband?

# The Biggest Do-It-Afraid Moment of my Life

Things were going pretty well with work and in my marriage. I was a different woman. I was happier and fulfilled and I had a sense of purpose. I was also able to be the kind of mother I wanted my children to have. I was able to do school runs, to drop my children off at school and pick them up after school, a luxury I hadn't been able to afford in my past life.

Things were pretty good until I began to feel a prompting in my spirit to tell my husband what had happened. I felt it strongly but I was petrified. Just thinking about telling him would lead me to tears.

Lord, how would he take it?

I had just started the second discipleship course at church, called, Experiencing God. It was the first week, and our classes held in the evening. I had spent the afternoon crying at the thought of telling my husband when I got up and decided to go to class. My husband, who didn't know what was going on, insisted on taking me. By God-incidence, that same day, he joined the discipleship class.

After dropping me off, he had left to go to a party on the other side of town. On his way, he saw that the car tyre was low, so he drove back to the island to get it checked. By the time he was done, he decided that there was no point going all the way back and so he just waited for me to finish my class.

When I had walked into class, the leader asked me about my husband and why he wasn't joining the class. I told him he wasn't interested; he hadn't even done the first discipleship course, which was a prerequisite to taking this second course.

Toward the end of that day's class, I walked out to call my husband and find out where he was and I saw him in the reception waiting for me. I asked him to come into the class because we were celebrating a fellow course mate's birthday and there was a lot to eat and drink, but he said he wasn't interested; he was going to take a tour of the church building instead. When I got back into the class I mentioned that my husband had been waiting for me but he wouldn't come in. The leader of the class asked where he was and went to talk to him. He invited him to the class. Protocols were broken on his behalf and he joined the same class I was in.

That's how my husband's spiritual journey started.

My husband had given his life to Christ at a very young age, he even had a vision of Jesus when he was a child but when he moved to England things changed a bit, and I had prayed for many years for my husband to begin to seek a deeper relationship with God.

In hindsight, I realise God had been working all the while. But as God was working, the devil too was trying his best to distract me from being the soil my husband needed. God had actually started working on my husband from the very first day I started fasting and praying for him, and the devil had been fighting it just as hard – it was when I'd started fasting weekly for him that the temptations had started. In fact, the first time my husband called to tell me he had paid his tithe was the first day Mr Temptation and I started chatting. My husband had never believed in the concept of tithing so the fact that he called to say he had paid his tithe had completely baffled me.

And now, through all my temptations, just like that, he was doing the discipleship course! Hmm, I was in awe of God.

As at today, he has done all three discipleship courses.

Here I was worried about telling him and then that same day he joined the discipleship course. I was confused but I was also excited for what God was doing.

In the Experiencing God course, we're taught that God is the One at work. When He shows you where He is at work, it's an invitation to join Him.

I saw that God was at work in my husband's life.

With the benefit of hindsight, I have come to realise that God was preparing me to tell my husband what had happened, and at the same time he was preparing my husband for the journey ahead. So I began to watch.

The promptings became stronger. I remember sharing it with my Pastor and another church leader and they both said they didn't think it was time to tell him. My Pastor said he didn't think my husband was ready to receive such news; our marriage was still recovering. But I knew God had told me to tell Him. I cried every time I felt God was prompting me, but then I started to rationalise the entire incident. After all, it's not like I slept with him. And besides, God was blessing me. Maybe the reason the whole thing happened was so I could work in church.

One particular day I received a prophecy from a lady saying, "Be bold, to take a step of faith. Trust Him. God said, 'I'll be right there with you'."

Another day I was at a prayer gathering, and in the midst of the prayer someone prophesied and said, "There's someone here, God has asked you to do something but the leaders of the church have said you shouldn't. You must do it. Destiny is involved."

It was surreal, but I knew God was speaking to me. I took this as confirmation that it was time to tell him, but I didn't know how I was going to. How was I even supposed to start?

I prayed to God for guidance and He asked me to write. It was an, *'aha!'* moment; I express myself better when I write and it was truly the best way to have broken the news to him. Thank God I went back to ask Him how He wanted me to do it.

So I wrote a very long message and saved it on my phone. One night, around 1 am, I felt a strong urge to send it.

Finally, I did.

I went to the movie room to see him. I told him we had to talk. He said we should wait till morning and I told him I had sent him an email.

My husband didn't come to bed that night. I couldn't sleep; it was the longest night of my life.

When it was dawn I went to meet him. He had read my email. He asked me if that was all that happened and I said yes. He asked if I was certain and I said yes. I was in tears.

He left the movie room and walked to our bedroom. And then he walked to the dressing room. I knelt down and looked up as though I was looking at God and cried. I followed him into the room. And then he did the strangest thing. He hugged me and he prayed for me. Yes, he prayed for me.

He didn't scream, shout, kick me out, or anything other thing you would think a man would do.

I told him I was really sorry. He asked why I didn't tell him when I found out 'temptation' was going to be in the same country as I was. I said I was scared. He said I should have told him, he said he would have helped me fight it.

Till today I am in awe of what God did that day. I don't know where my husband found the strength to react that way but it can only be God. God covered him.

I am eternally grateful to God and to him.

Our marriage has been through its fair share of trials but, like the palm tree, we have bounced back stronger. These are the best days of our marriage. We celebrated 10 years of being married on the 24th of June, 2016, and my husband asked us to renew our vows. He also had a surprise dinner for me afterwards to mark my 35th birthday.

I had expected the worst. I was also afraid that some of the things that happened the first time, such as the accidents and emotional trauma, would happen again, but it's like the entire incident never even happened. When my friend was getting married recently, I was reluctant to go to her wedding because I felt that she had put my marriage at risk and, as my friend, she should have protected me even from my own self. But when I told my husband I didn't want to go for her wedding, he insisted I forgive her and ensured that we went to the wedding together.

This is a man who I'd thought would either opt for a divorce or make me suffer, but God just covered him and gave him the grace to forgive me.

Our society expects men to cheat and not women. Women forgive men when they cheat but it is almost unheard of for a man to forgive a woman for cheating.

Actually, society makes us believe that women don't cheat and it is only men who do, but this is not the case. More women are cheating now, especially in the work environment.

My husband is a rare man and, truly, the grace of God is over him. I am still in awe and almost disbelief.

God has also blessed us tremendously; all that was lost has been restored.

On both our ends, doors have opened and we are living 'the Richer life'. Truly, like my mum said before I got married, "it is God who blesses." He has blessed us.

My husband is earning so much more than I am, and through this process I have learnt respect and humility. It actually doesn't even matter who is earning more or less, we are one and God can choose to bless us anyway He chooses.

I read the book 'Redeeming Love' by Francine Rivers and I have felt that love.

I've experienced that love from my husband; the love he has for me is a 'Redeeming Love'. I can't understand it. It can only be God. I thank God that he is being obedient to God's call on his life. I don't deserve the kind of love my husband shows me. He takes care of me and provides for me. He allows me to take on big, scary projects, like the conferences I have hosted, even at our own expense. He supports me and is committed to ensuring that I fulfil God's purpose for my life.

I have experienced the Love of God that completely baffles me. Why He stopped me from sleeping with that man, I still don't understand. Many women have done it – many are still doing it – but for some reason, He stopped me. I can't understand that kind of love. He didn't have to. Even if I had gone ahead to sleep with him, He would still have forgiven me, but for some reason He chose not to.

Oh, I cannot comprehend the love of God. I'm so thankful for His love.

If you're a lady reading this and you have given in to temptation, please do not despair. There is nothing God cannot do. You have to first of all repent and bring all your burdens to Him; ask Him to help you. He will help you like He helped me.

My entire life has turned around. I'm living the life that I longed for and prayed for. I get to spend time with my children, and they are excelling in school and character. My marriage is renewed and my husband and I are back to being best of friends. We are in love. We are thriving financially; God has blessed and opened so many doors for the two of us. I also have a successful career doing what I love, what I'm passionate about, and I work from home. I'm not just working, but I'm working in purpose.

# The Birth of This Book

I felt a strong urge to write a book, I even saw a vision of me writing a book. But instead of asking God what kind of book He wanted me to write, I assumed it had to be a book on "Do It Afraid" and I started writing.

Then God began to prompt me to share my life story, to share everything.

I fought it hard, mainly because of the stigma for my husband and my children. What would my husband think? All his friends would find out that his wife cheated on him. What about my kids? What about my in-laws? What about the church? I prayed about it and, when I told my husband what God had said, he gave me his full permission. I also told my Pastor and he said I should go ahead.

Still, I procrastinated. I thought, maybe it's for the future. But in December 2016, I had a speaking engagement at Google and a lady who I had never met in my life walked up to me and said, "You are writing a book. God said it must be birthed quickly. I see Q1 of 2017. This book will save numerous marriages. It will speak specifically to young wives. I am reminded of the time when women of old would go to the streams with the younger women and they would chat whilst doing whatever they went to the stream to do. During these conversations, knowledge is shared by the older women with the younger ones, albeit informally. However, these conversations save homes, build women and so on. This is what your book will do to many homes. A lot of young women are suffering in silence and are lost with no real teachers from older women to direct them. Your book will save homes and marriages..."

After this message I decided I was going to go ahead and be obedient, I was going to write my story. Then the series of challenges began.

That very week, my second daughter was diagnosed with bilateral inguinal hernia. I took out the rest of the month of December to seek God's will concerning her and to pray for her, then I decided to take out the month of January to seek God's face and write the book.

In January, we went through a series of attacks, which were targeted at my children, back to back. My oldest daughter was diagnosed with a knee condition that required her to wear a cast for two weeks. She broke her toe on the same day we were going to put the cast on her knee. The day we were meant to remove her cast, I got a call that I should rush home because a heavy metal pole had fallen on my second daughter's head – the same one who needed surgery. She had to get stitched.

My son fell and hit his head twice, my nanny had a really random bad allergic reaction from an insect bite, some days later she couldn't move one side of her body and had malaria and typhoid.

All these things were happening back to back. In fact, even a parent and teachers at my kids' school began to speculate and say that I needed to pray fervently.

Initially, I was afraid, but I realised that these things were all distractions. The devil clearly didn't want me to write this book. Immediately after an attack, my resolve would strengthen and I would write for hours. Those attacks actually acted as catalysts and helped me focus. The devil didn't know that I was being refreshed in the process.

In the process of writing this book, my second daughter and I had to fly abroad for surgery, which was successful to the glory of God. The day we were getting ready for the surgery, we were told she had a tiny murmur in her heart. Again, I was initially scared, but God reminded me to resist the devil. Instead I decided to believe that the murmur they heard was the heartbeat of the Holy Spirit living in her. We checked it out and the doctor said her heart is perfect, to the glory of God.

This book is clearly going to have a huge impact in our generation and that is why the devil has tried so hard to stop it.

I love the Lyrics to the song *Broken Vessels (Amazing Grace)* by Hillsong Worship, it speaks a lot about my life. I am that broken vessel I spoke about earlier, the one who wanted to be perfect so it could serve the King. But God has used me and blessed me, even in my brokenness. Like Rick Warren said, "In God's garden of grace even a broken tree can bear fruit."

Is there anything in your past that is keeping you from fulfilling God's purpose for you? Do you feel like God can't use you because of your past?

Give it all to God. He has redeemed you.

# PART 2:
# *The Richer Woman*

# Who is the Richer Woman?

This book is written for women who desire to have true wealth, and not just money.

Women who want to know how to live a purpose-filled life.

Women who want to live a life of purpose but can't, for several reasons – including fear.

Women who want to follow their dreams, not a pay check.

Women who want to be the best mothers to their kids and the best wives to their spouses.

Women who don't want to compromise on family in pursuit of their career – women who also who don't want to give up on their God given dreams because of their families.

Women who have a past and feel like God can't use them.

Women who don't want to give up on their marriage.

Women who want to be the epitome of all God created us to be.

Women who want to be successful in every facet of life.

Let us look at who that woman is, as described in the Bible in **Proverbs Chapter 31**:

*Who can find a virtuous and capable wife?*
*She is more precious than rubies.*

*Her husband can trust her;*
*and she will greatly enrich his life*

*She brings him good and not harm,*
*All the days of her life.*

*She finds wool and flax,*
*And busily spins it.*

*She is like a merchant's ship,*
*Bringing her food from afar.*

*She gets up before dawn to prepare breakfast*
*for her household,*
*And plan the day's work for her servant girls.*

*She goes to inspect a field and buys it;*
*With her earnings she plants a vineyard.*

*She is energetic and strong,*
*a hard worker.*

*She makes sure her dealings are profitable*
*And her lamp burns late into the night.*

*Her hands are busy spinning thread,*
*Her fingers twisting fiber.*

*She extends a helping hand to the poor,*
*And opens her arms to the needy.*

*She has no fear of winter for her household,*
*For everyone has warm clothes.*

*She makes her own bedspreads;*
*She dresses in fine linen and purple gowns.*

*Her husband is well known at the city gates,*
*Where he sits with other civic leaders.*

*She makes belted linen garments,*
*And sashes to sell to the merchants.*

*She is clothed with strength and dignity;*
*And she laughs without fear of the future.*

*When she speaks her words are wise,*
*And she gives instructions with kindness.*

*She carefully watches everything in her household,*
*And suffers nothing from laziness.*

*Her children stand and bless her;*
*Her husband praises her:*

*"There are many virtuous and capable women in the world,*
*But you surpass them all."*

*Charm is deceptive, and beauty does not last,*
*But a woman who fears the Lord, will be greatly praised.*
*Reward her for all she has done,*
*Let her deeds publicly declare her praise.*
**Proverbs 31:10-31 (NLT)**

I once pursued money.

I was focused on being a successful career woman at the expense of other areas of my life. Now, I realise that all I want is to live a life of purpose. I want to be successful in every single area of my life, and not just one area. I want to excel at every gift and responsibility God has given me.

I no longer want to pursue my own dreams and goals or my own purpose; I want to pursue God's purpose for me.

The Proverbs 31 woman is the epitome of a woman of purpose; she doesn't compromise on her family in pursuit of a career.

How do I know this?

1. She is a very successful and industrious woman, a woman who has businesses, who invests, who uses her wealth wisely:

   *"She goes to inspect a field and buys it;*
   *With her earnings she plants a vineyard.*

   *She makes sure her dealings are profitable*

   *She makes belted linen garments and sashes to sell to the merchants."*

2. She is fashionable:

   *"She dresses in fine linen and purple gowns."*

3. She takes care of herself, and is healthy:

   *"She is energetic and strong, a hard worker."*

4. She loves the Lord:

   *"But a woman who fears the Lord will be greatly praised."*

5. She has a great relationship with her husband and she helps him achieve his vision:

> *"Her husband can trust her and she will greatly enrich his life."*

> *"Her husband is well known at the city gates where he sits with the other civic leaders."*

6. She's a great mother:

> *"Her children stand and bless her. Her husband praises her."*

7. She is a praying woman:

> *"Her lamp burns into the night.""*.

This is the kind of woman I would love to be; the kind of woman I pray I become. This is the "Richer Woman".

The picture of the Richer Woman may seem intimidating. It's hard enough being a career woman or being a mother on its own, but being able to combine all the roles without dropping the ball? Being able to be the perfect mother, perfect wife, perfect businesswoman or perfect employee, all at the same time?

It doesn't only seem impossible, it seems like an unfair demand for anyone to place on an individual.

The Richer Woman isn't "perfect". She's not flawless. The Bible never said, "She is perfect," neither does it say, "She doesn't have a past". Sometimes, she's a broken vessel who God wants to use to carry out His perfect will. Like me, the process can be lengthy and full of challenges, but once we surrender to Him, He will use all our flaws to fulfil His perfect purpose. And that's when we start to become the Richer Woman. I am becoming the Richer Woman.

The first step to surrendering to God is to understand our roles – our function – as women, on earth. Who are we? What were we created for? What are we supposed to do?

Our primary roles are: first, our role as daughters of the Most High God, second, our role as wives to our husbands and, third, our role as mothers to our children. Our careers come *after* these primary roles.

Just before you roll your eyes and ask, "But what about the men?" It's the same for them, as well. And, just the same way some men wrongly put money and career first, a lot of women compromise on the first three roles to God, spouse and children, in the pursuit of money or careers – just like I did in the past.

Let us examine these three important roles.

# Role as the Father's Daughter

*"But a woman who fears the Lord will be greatly be praised."*
**Proverbs 31:30 NIV**

What comes to your mind when you hear the phrase, "the Father's daughter"?

Have you ever had someone say to you, "You look familiar, what is your name?" And when you say your first name, they ask you for your surname. And when you tell them, they say, "Yes! You are ...'s daughter!"

It's the same with God.

We are, first of all, daughters of the Most High God. He is our Creator and our Father.

To know the Father's daughter, you first have to know the Father. In order to know who you are and what you are worth, you have to know who your Father is.

## Who Is The Father?

Answer: God.

**Who is God? Who is God to *you*?**

One of my favourite songs is, **Good Good Father by Chris Tomlin**. The song title says it all; :

**God is a good good Father.**

He is my best friend. He is my Father. He is my lover. He is the Father of fathers, a Father to the fatherless. This means so much to someone like me, who didn't have the kind of father-daughter relationship I needed or desired.

I have seen the Father's love. He is the King of kings. He is the Lord of lords. He is the creator of the universe. He is the greatest lover, the greatest musician, the greatest artist, architect, engineer, mathematician, doctor, the Greatest everything!

Sometime ago, while watching Animal Planet, I marvelled at how intelligent animals are, even the tiniest of them all. How can a small ant create a massive anthill as tall as a human being? Have you seen how beautiful birds are, or the wonderful colours of all the creatures, even the snake? Do you know how magnificent and intelligent an eagle is? My Father created all these.

Who is the richest man in the world? Bill Gates? Well, my Father created him, even the King of Saudi Arabia. My Father is the King of kings; therefore I am a princess of princesses.

My Father does not care about my mistakes. He loves me despite my mistakes. In fact, I can say that the more mistakes or shortcomings I have, the deeper His love for me, and His strength is made perfect in my weaknesses.

Look at the lineage of Christ; it is filled with broken women. Rahab was a prostitute, Ruth a widow, Tamar an idol worshipper, Bathsheba an adulteress and Mary a peasant girl. After the resurrection, Jesus's first appearance was to Mary, a prostitute. Even the great men of the Bible had their own brokenness. Moses was a murderer, David an adulterer and murderer, Solomon a womanizer, Noah got drunk, Abraham lied and slept with his maid, Peter denied Jesus three times, Paul persecuted Christians, and it goes on and on! It doesn't matter if you have been raped, abandoned, abused, beaten, molested or cheated on, have HIV/AIDS, committed abortions, slept with married men, had multiple sleeping partners, a prostitute, a lesbian, or a transsexual. He loves you just the way you are. It is your heart He is looking at.

Don't get me wrong; I'm not saying these things are right. I'm saying, your past, your struggles or weaknesses do not determine His love for you. He loves you just the way you are and He wants you to come to Him just as you are. He wants you to lay all your burdens at His feet and repent.

*For God did not send His son into the world to condemn the world, but that the world through Him night be saved."*
**John 3:17 NKJV**

I love the song, Come to the River by House Fires II. It talks about God's heart for us. God longs for us to come to Him to receive grace, mercy, forgiveness, and His Love.

So now that you have a tiny idea of who the Father is, who is His daughter?

## The Father's Daughter

*"Who can find a virtuous and capable wife? She is more precious than rubies."*
**Proverbs 31:10 NIV**

Let us look at the Ruby:

Rubies are one of the most sought after gemstones in the world. Natural rubies are extremely rare in large sizes. The large ones can demand higher prices than diamonds.

The Ruby is one of the most beautiful gemstones created by nature. It is either pinkish red or deep, rich red colour. Corundum, which rubies are made from, is one of the hardest substances known to man and is second in hardness only to diamonds.

Rubies were worn by Kings or aristocrats since the dawn of time.

Almost all rubies have flaws, and the Ruby is a gemstone that represents the passion of love.[4]

God says you are worth far more than a ruby. In fact, He didn't just say *a* ruby; He said **many** rubies. You are highly valuable to God.

Like most rubies you may have flaws, but remember that rubies without imperfections are very rare. In fact, the imperfections of the ruby are used to identify the authenticity of the stones![5] And, just like rubies go through a heating process, you will go through tests and trials to improve your character.

---

[4] "Ruby." My Stone Gems. Retrieved January 18, 2017, from http://www.mystonegem.com/ruby-2/

"Ruby Facts: Interesting Information about Rubies." 25Karats.Com. Retrieved January 18, 2017, from https://www.25karats.com/education/gemstones/ruby

[5] "All natural rubies have imperfections in them, including color impurities and inclusions of rutile needles known as "silk". Gemologists use these needle inclusions found in natural rubies to distinguish them from synthetics, simulants, or substitutes."

"Ruby: Physical Properties" Wikipedia. Retrieved January 22, 2017, from https://en.wikipedia.org/wiki/Ruby

# The Father's Love

> *"I have loved you with an everlasting love."*
> **Jeremiah 31:3 NIV**

> *"For God so loved the world that He gave His only begotten Son, that whoever believes in Him should not perish but have everlasting life."*
> **John 3:16 ESV**

See, you are not an accident. God made you so that He could love you.

He wasn't lonely – He had Jesus and the Holy Spirit and there's already perfect love in the Holy Trinity. But He wanted to make you in order to express His love for you.

> *He has carried us since we were born. He has taken care of us from our birth. Even when we are old He will be the same. Even when our hair has turned grey; He will take care of us. I made you, and I will care for you. I will carry you along and save you.*
> **Isaiah 46:4 NLT**

Like a ruby, your scars make you valuable. Look at Joyce Meyer who was abused by her own father repeatedly. God used all her trials to shape her heart, and she has made such a huge impact in God's Kingdom. Everything you've gone through is for a purpose.[6]

---

[6] "God made us for a reason and our life has profound meaning. We discover that meaning and purpose when we make God the reference point of our lives."

– Rick Warren, from *The Purpose Driven Life*.

# The Father's Single Daughter

In the description of the ruby, it says, "Rubies were worn by kings or aristocrats since the dawn of time."[7]

In the royal family of old, a king was meant to marry someone of royal ancestry.

You are the daughter of the King of kings, the daughter of the Most High God. You must marry and align with royalty. This doesn't mean you must seek money or perfection; Royalty refers to royal blood – the blood of Jesus that He shed for us – and not money. You must align with a man after God's own heart, because a man after God's own heart is the Father's son, the son of the King of kings.

If you're a young lady reading this, you don't have to pawn your sexuality in order to attract love. You don't have to do anything at all but be who you were created to be. Just like a ruby, you will shine as long as you stay true to your identity as the Father's daughter and remain in your place of purpose.

I came across a poem by Russel Kelfer, titled, "You Are Who You Are", in the book, The Purpose Driven Life. It talks about how everything about us was perfectly designed by God for a reason. It is quite profound. It is as follows:

*You are who you are for a reason*
*You are part of an intricate plan*
*You are a precious and perfect unique design*
*Called God's special woman.*

*You look like you look for a reason*
*Our God made no mistake*

---

[7] "Ruby." My Stone Gems. Retrieved January 18, 2017, from http://www.mystonegem.com/ruby-2/

*He knit you together within the womb*
*You are just what He wanted to make.*

*The parents you had were the ones He chose*
*And no matter how you may feel*
*They were custom designed with God's plan in mind.*
*And they bear the Masters seal.*

*No, that trauma you faced wasn't easy*
*And God wept that it hurt you so,*
*But it was allowed to shape your heart.*
*So that into His likeness you'd grow.*

*You are who you are for a reason*
*You've been formed by the Master's rod.*
*You are who you are, beloved*
*Because there is a God.*

**Russel Kelfer.**

Flowers blossom and attract bees. They don't worry about how the bee will find them. They stay in their place of purpose. You were created exactly as you are for a purpose, and you don't need to compromise your identity in your search for a romantic relationship.

I read a story about how Mohammed Ali taught his daughters about their value. He told them that all precious things God created – like diamonds, gold and pearls – are all hidden. Gold and diamonds are covered by heaps of rocks while pearls are found at the bottom of the sea.

To find these precious stones you must understand their value, and be willing to go the extra mile to find them – and these ones are not even as valuable as rubies! This means we must remain covered up.

At some point in my life I thought I had to dress a certain way to look beautiful and attract men. I learnt the hard way that that only attracts the wrong kinds of men. Don't get me wrong, I'm not saying you should dress drab and ugly and unattractive. You can protect your precious, valuable, private property that is reserved for your better half and still be fashionable and beautiful. After all, God is very interested in fashion. He was after all the first fashion designer:

> *Also for Adam and his wife the Lord God made tunics of skin, and clothed them.*
> **Genesis 3:21 NKJV**

Men go to great lengths to find a ruby. They dig mines for years and years. What more will they do to find someone who is worth more than rubies? A man finds his wife, while a woman chooses her husband. You don't have to do anything but be found.

You may be thinking, "But my time is far spent!" or, "I don't want to wait to be found!" Trust me, like Ruth, when you're focused on fulfilling God's purpose for you, your Boaz will come looking for you.

God has kept nothing but the best for you. The Bible says:

> *If you then, being evil, know how to give good gifts to your children, how much more will your Father who is in Heaven give good things to those who ask Him.*
> **Mathew 7:11 NKJV**

As a single lady, you have a lot of time to dedicate to

bonding with your Father who is your first love. When you marry, you will be so consumed with being a wife and mother that sometimes you will crave this alone time with the Lord. Maximise it. Serve Him and find your purpose.

## The Fathers daughter and the sunflower

One day, on my way to work, I felt led to do some research on the beautiful plant called the sunflower. I was expecting to learn something new about God because the Bible says,

> *"The heavens declare the glory of God; the skies proclaim the work of his hands. Day after day they pour forth speech; night after night they display knowledge."*
> **Psalm 19:1-2 WEB**

However, I didn't expect to learn something so phenomenal.

The sunflower is a beautiful plant. It looks like the sun. It is often given as a gift to cheer people up. It is regarded as the happiest plant and is also regarded as a loyal plant.

The sunflower has very many uses. Its seeds are eaten as a tasty snack. The seeds also produce sunflower oil, which can be used for cooking, to make margarine or for salads. You can also make flour from sunflower seeds, which can be used to bake. Sunflower oil can also be used to make cosmetic products like shampoo, lip balm, and lotions. The stalk of a sunflower can also be used to make paper. Sunflower seeds are eaten by animals and birds as food, and the sunflower is also a bee's delight as it produces a lot of honey.

Now, these are wonderful features, however what makes the sunflower so special is what I'm about to share next.

When a sunflower is still growing, it follows the sun. Its stalk grows toward the light and, during the day, it turns to follow the movement of the sun.

When it reaches maturity, i.e. when the flowers are in full bloom, it stops turning towards the sun and faces east permanently.

I wondered why it stopped tracking the sun in its maturity and also why it's faces the east, so I did some more research and realised that the sun rises from the East and sets in the West.

So, when the sunflower is mature, rather than turning constantly in search of the sun, it already knows where the sun rises from and decides to face that direction permanently.

This is quite deep, and I'll explain why. Here's what we can learn from this peculiar habit of the Sunflower:

As we human beings grow in our lives on earth, we ought to follow the Son. We ought to look to the Son for sustenance and for growth. Without the Son we will wither and die and never reach full potential, we will never bloom. But as we follow the Son, we will reach our full potential. We will grow; we will blossom. By the time we reach full maturity and we are blooming, we already know the Son based on our relationship in our growth years. Therefore, like the sunflower does when it reaches maturity by facing east where the sun rises, we must face the Son permanently and rest in His presence. Once morning comes, because we are in alignment with the Son, we are immediately immersed in His presence. And when we die, we continue in His presence in eternity.

The Son I am referring to is the Lord Jesus Christ, the Son of God who is God himself. Without Him, we are nothing.

> *I am the vine, you are the branches. He who abides in Me, and I in him, bears much fruit; for apart from Me you can do nothing.*
> **John 15:5 (ESV)**

Without Him we can't have fulfilled lives. Without Him, we won't reach our full potential. Without Him we will wither and die.

With Him, we will live fulfilled lives. With Him we will bear fruit just like the Sunflower bears fruit. With Him we will bring joy to all who come in contact with us. We will bring light. With Him we will deepen our relationship and grow to love Him, we will remain in His presence in this life and the next.

As the Sunflower grows, darkness comes when there is no more sunlight. In the same way, there are moments in our lives where there is darkness.

While in the growth stage, the Sunflower is constantly turning in search of light. But in maturity, it knows that morning will definitely come and it's just a matter of time, so it waits and faces east permanently.

In the same way, we must grow into the level of maturity where we have hope that morning will come and God will be there, no matter how dark our circumstances appear to be. We must sit and wait for Him. We must sit in His presence.

I hope you are encouraged to turn towards the Son, to spend your life in pursuit of Him. That way you will have a fulfilled life and will be prosperous in every aspect of your life. You will live the abundant life. You will bear fruit and be a blessing to the world and you will remain with Him in eternity when you leave this temporary place.

## God's Purpose for His Married Daughters

> *"For I know the plans I have for you," says the Lord. "They are plans for good and not for disaster, to give you a future and a hope."*
> **Jeremiah 29:11 NLT**

God created us for a purpose. There's a mandate He wants us to run with; a dream and vision He wants us to accomplish. However, many women relegate this purpose in pursuit of careers that bring us financial fulfilment.

We want to be rich and successful. We want to wear the latest designer clothes, drive the nicest cars, carry the most expensive bags, travel first class and live the 'rich life'. We do this at the expense of other areas of our lives.

I was once like this. I wanted to be successful at all costs. I've had a series of dreams – at first I wanted to be the youngest female partner at the accounting firm I worked in, then I wanted to be Minister of Finance – and while there is nothing wrong with achieving these dreams, and while they could be considered great achievements, **this wasn't God's plan for me**. This wasn't the purpose He created me for. I could have pursued my dreams and been successful, but I would have failed the most important test which is what I was put on this earth to do.

See, if you want to know the purpose of a thing you have to ask the creator. I had no idea or dream to be in media. I didn't even know I was able to co-host a TV show. It was never on my list of goals, yet I am now a co-host on a talk show that airs in 44 African countries and the UK. That's why it is dangerous to follow new teachings that require you to follow your self-driven dreams. Instead, you should follow God's dreams for you and set goals according to God's plans.

I would have missed my purpose completely.

I remember listening to Christopher Kolade, a very successful man, speak and He said that all he'd ever wanted in his life was to be an educationist. He did this for five years. Subsequently, he decided to seek God's purpose and, as a result, he has been an ambassador to the UK, a director in different companies including one of the biggest FMCG (fast moving consumer goods) companies in Nigeria, amongst many other things. He would have missed out on all God had planned for him if he chosen to follow his own dream. By all means dream big, but make sure it is God's dream.

Ask yourself this: What is God's purpose and plan for you? Are you walking in it? If you aren't, take some time out to pray and seek God for direction.

I recently read the story of Folusho and Shade Ogunleye, the founders of Ice Cream Factory, the first of its kind in Nigeria. Folusho was a financial analyst who worked with Shell UK, while his wife Shade worked in accounting and management. They both took time out to seek God for a business idea to pursue. They had different business ideas and decided to fast and pray and seek God's face. God confirmed the idea to start Ice Cream Factory. They moved back to Nigeria and started their company.

Everything God created on earth has a purpose and fulfils its purpose. The fish in the sea, the birds in the sky, the plants on the earth, they all fulfil the purpose they were created to fulfil.

Man is the only being that was made in God's image. We have free will and, as a result, man is the only being that decides or chooses whether or not to fulfil his/her purpose. Men are becoming women; women becoming men, and women are pursuing careers that they were not born to fulfil. This must change.

If you don't have a love relationship with the Father, ask the Holy Spirit to bring you into that kind of wholehearted love relationship, a Father-daughter kind. If you don't know God and you want to make Jesus your Lord and Saviour, then please say this prayer:

> *"Lord Jesus, thank You for leading me to this point in my life and for being with me all of my life. I'm sorry for being far away from You and I'm sorry for all my sins. I repent of all my sins. Please forgive me, Lord. Please come into my heart and be my Lord and Saviour. I believe in You and the sacrifice You made for me on the cross of Calvary. I give You my life and I submit my will to You. Please help me to be more like You, to be obedient to You and please send me the Holy Spirit as my helper. Lord, I desire a Father-daughter relationship with You and I look forward to this love relationship. In Jesus Name, Amen."*

If you said this prayer, please ask God to lead you to a Bible-believing church. This will help with your spiritual growth. I would also suggest that you read the Bible, you can start from the Book of John.

If you are already saved, but desire a love relationship with the Father, then please say the prayer below:

> *"Father, I desire a Father-daughter, love relationship with You. I want to walk*

*intimately with You. I want to love You and be loved by You. Please lead me, guide me and help me to walk with You daily, every minute, every second, every moment of the day. I love You, Lord. In Jesus Name, Amen."*

# Role as a wife

*"Her husband can trust her, and
She will greatly enrich his life.
She brings him good, not harm, all the days of
her life."*

**Proverbs 31:11-12 NLT**

When I was reflecting and seeking an analogy that represents the woman and her role as a wife to her husband, the Lord led me to the soil.

A seed is a powerful element that has the potential to achieve great things, however, the soil that this seed is deposited into plays a big role in determining whether or not that seed reaches its potential. No matter how powerful or how much potential a seed has, it cannot flourish if it does not go into soil. Essentially, it is practically useless and unable to fulfil its purpose to become the plant it was created to be, without the soil. The quality and depth of the soil also determines whether the plant will survive or not.

Soil tends to have a richness that sand doesn't have[8]. It comes from organic matter being mixed into it. Organic matter refers to rock particles, humus, water and air. Soil is

---

[8] Carlson, Seth. "What is the different between soil and sand?" Quora. Retrieved September 23 2016, from https://www.quora.com/What-is-the-different-between-soil-and-sand

important to plants because it stores nutrients and serves as a medium for growth. It is an anchor for roots and also holds water needed by plants for moisture. Soil contains the air, water and food that provide a suitable place for plants to grow. A vital function of soil is storing and supplying minerals and nutrients that are essential for plant life.[9]

While reflecting on this, the Holy Spirit reminded me about the parable of the farmer in Matthew Chapter 13. This is a story of a farmer who scattered seed. Some fell on shallow soil, some on a footpath and some among thorns. They all perished, but the seeds that fell on fertile soil flourished. Verse 8 says, "Still other seeds fell on fertile soil, and they produced a crop that was thirty, sixty, and even a hundred times as much as had been planted!"

The key thing to also note in that parable is the word, "fertile." Soil can also be unsuitable for growth if it is not fertile, or if it is shallow.

In this analogy, the seed represents a husband, while the soil represents a wife. A woman nurtures a man and enables him to achieve his full potential, like the soil provides nutrients and water for the seed.

Soil has a richness that sand doesn't. I can therefore say that The Richer Woman is the fertile soil, while the rich woman can be regarded as sand.

A man who marries the right woman – the Richer Woman – will flourish and bear fruit. She will enable him to grow well. She will provide him with the right environment to flourish. She will provide him with spiritual nutrients through her prayers. She will encourage him, support him,

---

[9] "Why is soil important to plants?" Reference.com. Retrieved February 19, 2017, from https://www.reference.com/science/soil-important-plants-645a14d830ef75f2

and provide for him if she has to. She sees his potential and she enables him to reach it.

The seed has its own food storage called the endosperm, which it feeds on before it starts to receive nutrients from the soil.

The seed with its own endosperm is like a man with vision. The man must receive his vision from the Lord as the seed received its endosperm from the creator of the seed.

The good soil doesn't stunt the growth of the seed; it allows the seed to feed on its own endosperm and provides the nutrients when the seed needs it. This is what a woman does to a man.

When the seed becomes a plant and grows above the soil in all its splendour, for the world to see, those who know the truth remember that, when the seed was hidden, the soil provided all it needed so that it could blossom. That plant wouldn't be standing without the nurture of the soil.

When the plant is grown, it is the soil that holds its roots down, and allows it to receive water from the wellspring in the earth. Good soil receives water from the wellspring and doesn't depend on rain alone.

In the same way, a wife keeps her man grounded and also ensures that He is connected to the true source of water, which is the Holy Spirit.

Our role as wives is our second most important role.

We are created to be helpmates to our spouses. We are created to help them fulfil their vision for self and family. Our husbands' work on earth, their purpose and even their destinies are also connected to us, and our obedience.

# Purpose

A woman is good for a man.

I've been reading a book by Myles Munroe titled, "Understanding The Purpose And Power of Woman." It is a very profound book that I believe every woman must read. In it, Myles Munroe says that the first purpose of a woman is as an enhancer and a helper. He

In chapter 6 of the book, Myles Munroe discusses the woman's role as an enhancer.

> "As enhancer, the woman is a co-leader who shares his vision and works with him to accomplish what they were both created to do. The woman takes who the man is and what the man has and enlarges and extends it. In this way his leadership is effective and their shared vision becomes reality."

Myles Munroe shares that the first purpose of a woman as an enhancer is to be a companion for the male, so that he won't be alone.[10]

He also explains that a woman's role as an enhancer does not take away from her ability to have her own interests.[11]

---

[10] "As enhancer, the woman is a co-leader who shares his vision and works with him to accomplish what they were both created to do. The woman takes who the man is and what the man has and enlarges and extends it. In this way his leadership is effective and their shared vision becomes reality."

– Myles Munroe, from *Understanding The Purpose And Power of Woman*.

[11] "This certainly does not mean that a woman should not have her own interests and develop her own abilities. It means that, as a couple, they need to share the same vision for their lives."

– Myles Munroe, from *Understanding The Purpose And Power of Woman*.

I like the part where he says, "This certainly does not mean that a woman should not have her own interests and develop her own abilities. It means that, as a couple, they need to share the same vision for their lives."

So, in my case, my vision is to inspire people to live the "richer life". I could narrow it down to say it is to inspire women to be the "richer woman".

It is tied to my husband's vision: I cannot preach the message of the richer woman if I do not help my husband fulfil his vision. The richer woman is a woman who helps a man achieve his vision. I am focused on helping my husband achieve his vision of ensuring our kids have salvation and fulfil their purpose.

There was division when my vision was to be a rich woman and make money as fast as possible; our visions were not in alignment and in the pursuit of money, I wasn't able to spend time with our children, nurturing them to know Christ and develop their gifts and talents.

Finally Myles Munroe says as an enhancer:

> *"A woman is designed for the purpose of adapting to the man. This means that she has built -in energy and the built- in circuits to adapt to his vision and purpose."*
> *"Therefore, if a man wants a woman to adapt to him, he has to give her something to adapt to."*

If your husband doesn't have vision, pray to God to show him God's vision for him. If you don't know your husband's vision, then ask him.[12] My life changed the day I

---

[12] "A woman is designed for the purpose of adapting to the man. This means that she has built -in energy and the built- in circuits to adapt to his vision

realised that my purpose wasn't to make money but to help my husband fulfil his vision. For the first time after many years of marriage, about a year after I resigned from my job as an investment banker, we were at an event and he shared his vision with me. My sense of purpose has changed completely, since then. Being a good mother to his kids is part of me helping him achieve his vision.

Many marriages have failed because women neglected their roles. In fact, many women do not understand what their roles as wives actually require. This is largely due to the fact that we have seen negative examples from the generations before us.

Many of the women in our parents' generation were not allowed to work, and were completely at the mercy of their husbands. And many of the men in our parents' generation were strict, overbearing, and unsupportive. As a result of the cultural perspective where women were seen as property, many men did not respect their wives, and did not value their wives. This showed in the often-unfair ways a lot of the men treated them.

Due to this historical pattern, many of the women in our generation resolved not to repeat the same mistakes our parents did. We vowed to be independent, to make our own money, and to pursue success at all costs. Just like I did, many of us are chasing financial wealth because of the fears we have grown up with.

There's absolutely nothing wrong with having successful careers or being financially wealthy. The Proverbs 31 woman was successful, and so was her husband.

---

and purpose... Therefore, if a man wants a woman to adapt to him, he has to give her something to adapt to."

– Myles Munroe, from *Understanding The Purpose And Power of Woman*.

*"She makes sure her dealings are profitable..."*

*"Her husband is well known at the city gates, where he sits with the other civic leaders."*
**Proverbs 31:18, 23 NLT**

The problem only arises when we let our fears push us into making the wrong decisions, when we let our fears push us into putting our financial needs ahead of our spiritual and relational needs. Many of us weren't taught how to be good, loving wives to good, loving husbands, and so many of us don't even know that there's anything wrong with the way we're living life.

However, sooner or later, if we're honest with ourselves, we will admit that the pursuit of money isn't making us happy. Yes, many women say they have no choice but to pursue their career and neglect their husbands because their husbands are not "pulling their weight" and earning enough. Many women begin to resent their husbands because their husbands can't afford to give them the lifestyle they want. Many women are having affairs with their colleagues or with people they feel fit into their ideal "spec." Many women are depressed because they are bearing a load that they weren't made to bear.

As wives, we were created to help our husbands. We are made with the ideal set of skills to help build our husbands up. Whether it looks like it or not, your husband needs you - and he doesn't need you to put him down or belittle him, he needs you to bring out the King in him.

God places certain women in the lives of certain men to pray them up, encourage them and lift them up. After all there is a saying that goes, "behind every successful man is a woman." Men are wired to need the encouragement of their wives.

If you're a married woman reading this, if you're dissatisfied with your husband's ambition or income, has it ever occurred to you that maybe that is why God put you in his life in the first place? Maybe you are supposed to help him up.

Sometimes it's not that their husbands are lazy, but that the women want to live a certain lifestyle at all costs. Sometimes it is because of a need for security. You can call it instant satisfaction as against delayed gratification. As a result, they pursue certain careers and begin to resent their husbands. Their husbands, in return, become resentful and insecure.

It takes a lot of grace for a woman to respect a husband if she earns more money than he does. And a lot of the time, where there is resentment and insecurity, someone ends up having an extra marital affair, which is the beginning of the end of the marriage.

> *"Her husband is well known at the city gates, where he sits with the other civic leaders."*
> **Proverbs 31:23 NLT**

In Biblical times, kings and important people sat at the gates. The Proverbs 31 woman's husband was also influential, as he sat amongst the elders in the land.

Whenever I look at a successful woman, I look at her husband. If her husband too is successful, I smile, and I add her to my list of inspiring women.

Note: successful does not mean famous or rich. Success to me is someone fulfilling God's purpose for his or her life.

A sign of a successful woman who is living the "Richer" life is that she is successful in her pursuit of purpose – both as the Father's daughter and as a wife. And, following

Proverbs 31:23, I believe that one of the signs of being successful in our roles as wives is having successful husbands.

Again, this is not to say that women shouldn't have careers. By all means, do so! But not at the expense of your role as a wife; always remember your second, most-important role, which is your role as a wife. Always remember that your career is secondary.

In my case, my husband has shared his vision for our family with me and I try to help him achieve it as much as I can. I also try to pray for him daily in fulfilling God's purpose for his life. This also means I have to nurture his needs, which includes affirmation and also sex.

## Love and Sex

In the past, I was so busy at work that I had no time to meet my husband's needs. I neglected him. For a man, sex is so important, it is almost as important as food. Most women can live without sex for some time, especially when we have a lot on our minds: kids, work, finances. Because we don't always need it, it's easy for us to neglect our husbands, to withhold sex, or to use it as a bargaining tool.

It is important that we never deprive our husbands of sex; the word 'no' isn't an option. It is even a health issue. Sex reduces the risk of prostate cancer and heart disease in men, and it also reduces high blood pressure.

I know many women will protest this instruction. We spend long hours at work, rush home, take care of the kids and take care of the house while our husbands relax in front of the TV after work. Is it fair to also have to take care of him?

This comes back to our priorities and our understanding of our role as wives.

If we understand the power that we have as women to build or break our husbands lives, careers and even their relationships with God, we'll understand that we have a huge responsibility on our hands.

The reason we struggle to accept our role is that we're used to letting fear make our decisions for us. Fears like, "What if I always give him what he wants and he never returns the favour?" "What if I prioritise him over my career and he leaves me for another woman?" "If I always give him what he wants, he'll turn me into a doormat." "What if I trust him and he betrays my trust?"

I was once that woman who hid behind excuses. I earned a lot of money, I worked long hours, and I didn't have time to pander to my husband's needs. But once I understood who I was as the Father's daughter, once I stopped letting my fear of poverty control me; once I started walking in purpose and stopped being frustrated and unfulfilled all the time, I was able to fulfil my second role as a wife to my husband.

I also know that, as women, our bodies aren't always receptive to sex when we're not in the mood. I read a book once where the woman said, whenever her husband wants sex and she is not keen, she tells him to give her a few minutes to prepare and then she goes to the bathroom, to shower, spray perfume, wear nice lingerie – anything to help her get in the mood – and she also prays to God to help her, before she goes to meet her husband. Since you will have to account for your role as a wife when you meet God, you can also ask Him for help to fulfil every aspect of your role! It is not always easy, but thank God for our helper, the Holy Spirit.

## Finances

If you earn a lot more money than your husband, it is important to ensure that you don't let the state of your finances rule your home.

Like I said earlier, it takes a lot of grace for a woman to respect a husband she earns more than. It also takes a lot of grace for a man not to be intimidated by his wife's earnings.

I would advise that a woman who finds herself in this category be very intentional in her dealings with her husband. You must not disrespect him. He is the head of the home and this is not a function of his bank account. You must allow him to be the man and to make and take certain decisions. You must be submissive.

> *Wives, submit to your own husbands, as to the Lord. For the husband is head of the wife, as also Christ is head of the church; and He is the Saviour of the body. Therefore, just as the church is subject to Christ, so let the wives be to their own husbands in everything."*
> **Ephesians 5:22-24 NKJV**

> *Wives, likewise, be submissive to your own husbands, that even if some do not obey the word, they, without a word, may be won by the conduct of their wives, when they observe your chaste conduct accompanied by fear. Do not let your adornment be merely outwards - arranging the hair, wearing gold, or putting on fine apparel- rather let it be the hidden person of the heart, with the incorruptible beauty of a gentle and quiet spirit, which is very precious in the sight of God. For this manner, in former times, the holy women who trusted in God also*

> *adorned themselves, being submissive to their own husbands. As Sarah obeyed Abraham calling him lord, whose daughters you are if you do good and are not afraid with any terror."*
> **1 Peter 3:1-6 NKJV**

You must be very wise. Like the Bible says, be wise as a serpent and gentle as a dove. A formula that works is to let the man still take care of the major expenses of the home, while you save or invest your earnings for big and long-term goals for the family. I know a particular couple where the woman worked in a senior position and was earning a lot. Her husband too had a good job and they would save 100% of her earnings while they spent his earnings for their daily needs. Every year, they were able to go on really nice holidays as a family and they also were able to make very wise investment decisions. It allowed him to feel like the provider.

Currently, in my household, my husband does pretty much everything and I supplement whenever I need to or I can. He allows me to focus on my God-given assignments and He also supports me financially. He is my sponsor. This formula may not work for all, and there is no formula that is for all. It really depends on your peculiar situation as a family and what you decide works for both of you. You may decide to split it 50/50 or, in your situation, you may even have to do most of the providing. My point here is to emphasise that as a woman earning more than her spouse or contributing more financially, you have to be very careful not to disrespect your husband.

You may not even be earning more than your spouse, you may just be a very successful woman with a strong earning power, but you must be conscious as well.

I recall attending an event where Nigeria's foremost motivational speaker said that his wife might be a tiger in her workplace but, when she comes home, she is like a kitten and falls into his arms. Now that is an intentional woman.

As women, we must be careful not to make our husbands feel like they are not needed. Even if you can fix it, let him help you fix it. For example, don't just call the mechanic to fix your car, tell your husband your car isn't working and that you would like it if he could help you sort it out. This may just require him to call the mechanic, even if you end up paying for it. Like the Bible says in Matthew 10:16, *"Be wise as a serpent and gentle as a dove."*

Let him be the King and you, the Queen. There is a trend on social media where a lot of women like to call themselves Kings. What's wrong with being a Queen? We should be perfectly secure in our God-given roles and not try to contend for our husbands' roles.

Men are men and it is in their DNA to be respected.

> *Nevertheless, let each one of you in particular so love his own wife as himself, and let the wife see that she respects her husband.*
> **Ephesians 5:32 NKJV**

Some women may say, "But the Bible says men must love their wives too, and so how can I respect a man who doesn't love me?" To that I say, do your part and leave the rest to God. You are not in control of another person's actions; you are only in control of your own actions. The Bible promises that even these difficult husbands will be won by our conduct.

> *Wives, likewise, be submissive to your own husbands, that even if some do not obey the word, they, without a word, may be won by the*

> *conduct of their wives, when they observe your chaste conduct accompanied by fear.*
> **1 Peter 3:1-2 NKJV**

The Bible promises that even these difficult husbands will be won by our conduct.

## Prayer

A woman must also spend a lot of time praying for her husband. I remember once a Pastor in my church said, "Omi, your knees are not black enough. They should be black from you praying for your husband." That was an exaggeration, but the idea is clear: we must pray for our husbands every day.

There is so much to pray about. Men go through so much, and they need our prayers. Women have support systems, groups, and associations. There are so many women's seminars, but rarely do men get the chance to meet or interact. They go through a lot of their problems by themselves, and even when they have friends, rarely do they share and open up to them.

Our prayers are so important.

A book that helps me pray for my husband is the book, *The Power Of A Praying Wife* by Stormie Omartian. There are thirty different chapters, one for each day of the month. Periodically, I pray these chapters over and over again for my husband.

Some of the prayer points include his Wife (yes, *you*), his work, his finances, his sexuality, his affection, his temptations, his mind, his fears, his purpose, his choices, his health, his protection, his trials, and his fatherhood.

Stormie Omartian, who has been married for over 30 years, also shares some of the challenges she went through in her marriage as well as the experiences of other married couples. That book is a must-have.

I must warn you that, as you begin to pray for your husband, God will begin to show you areas where you also need to work on yourself.

There are also other books in the collection, including, *The Power Of Prayer To Change Your Marriage*, and, *The Power Of A Praying Husband*. I suggest you buy that one for your husband. Don't force him to read it; what I did was just place a copy of the book by my husband's bedside and, one day, God led him to open it up and pray for me without my having to say anything.

## Choosing a Husband

It is true that some men have character flaws. Ideally, for us women, we must ensure that we are intentional, observant and intuitive in our choice of spouse.

If you're a single woman reading this, you must spend time during the dating or courtship period to see if there are any character traits that you do not like.

As a single woman, it is important to marry a man who is secure in himself, a man who won't be intimidated by your success. It is important to marry a man who will be your greatest cheerleader and support. With this, you can soar to any heights in your career. This is what I always wanted in a man and I thank God He answered my prayers.

As I reread quotes from TD Jakes' book, *The Lady Her Lover and Her Lord*, the Holy Spirit explained to me why he had delayed my relationship with Mr Mysterious – my husband.

Even though I had already met him, I still went through the cycles of bad relationships with other people before we eventually started dating and then got married.

The Holy Spirit explained to me that He needed me to see myself in a different way before I could start dating the man who would become my husband. So, while my husband was preparing for his exams and didn't have time to pursue me, God was working on *me*, revealing my needy relationship patterns to me, and teaching me my true identity – even through the hurt and pain I experienced with other men.[13]

If you're single and you're wondering why God seems to be delaying your marriage, press into the Holy Spirit, ask Him to reveal your true self to you. It's only when you start to recognise your value as the Father's daughter that you'll be truly ready to step into your role as a wife.

This brings me to the subject of abuse. A woman who is abused – whether physically, emotionally or verbally – should get help. A man who does this to a woman has psychological problems and needs help. Please do not put your life in danger all in the name of submission and respect. If you are being abused, please separate yourself from the situation so you can get help for yourself and your husband. Too many women have been killed.

Note: I didn't say divorce, I said separate.

Do you have to be married to be considered successful? No. Do you have to be married to be considered an inspiration? No.

---

[13] Sometimes God delays relationships to give you a chance to heal as an individual. Then and only then can you make choices that are healthy--choices that are not predicated on obsessive need or fear of being alone. There are many people who endure unthinkable abuse because they are terribly afraid of being alone! To avoid themselves, they choose life with an abuser rather than a night at home alone. But there are some things that are worse than being alone."

– TD Jakes, from *The Lady, Her Lover and Her Lord.*

But for those who are married, and for those who desire to be married, it is important to understand that our roles as wives means that we are to help our husbands fulfil and achieve their God-given dreams and purposes.

This does not mean your husband must be popular or rich, it just means that even if his dreams are not financially motivated, even if his God-given purpose will not bring great monetary riches, we must still do all we can to enable this vision become a reality.

It is not easy, but we have the Holy Spirit our helper.

It is important for me to highlight that there is no perfect man. The grass is also not greener on the other side and if it is, it is because it has been watered well and taken care of. So, water your grass. Remember you are the soil that the grass depends on.

It is also important for me to say that you can't change anyone, only God can – and trust me, He can change **anyone**. He holds the hearts of Kings in His hands. He holds your husband's heart. There is no situation God cannot turn around.

# Role as a Mother

*"Her children stand and bless her"*
**Proverbs 31:28 NLT**

*"Children are a gift from the Lord, they are a reward from Him.""*.
**Psalm 127:3 NLT**

Many people will give anything to be able to give birth to their own children. Not all women do but, whether by birth or by adoption, being a mother is a gift and a privilege. Children are a gift from God, and it is our duty to be the best mothers we can be to our children.

Unfortunately, many women outsource their parenting to house helps, nannies, caretakers and day cares. I left my job when my first daughter was five and, prior to that, my nanny spent more time with her than I did.

They say the first ten years are vital to a child's development; some studies even say it's the first five years, and to think I spent those years prioritising my career over my family. This is one of the reasons I was so eager to resign by the time she turned five. Thankfully, my mum was always around and my husband was also very hands-on, however my daughter didn't get the best of me in her early years.

There is no amount of success you can have if your children are not brought up well.

I recently heard of a crèche that closes at 10pm. Imagine a child being picked up from crèche at that time of the night, what time would the child get home? What time would the child spend with his/her parents?

This is the case in many homes in our society. Many children do not see their parents for days because of how focused the parents are on pursuing financial wealth. Many young girls are sexually abused because their parents are absent. I know a woman who was raped by different people as a child. Her mother was absent from her life and the cook, driver and teacher all raped her.

Children are simple and all they want is time. Time is given to us by God for free, but unfortunately a lot of children can't afford to pay for their parents' time. Parents try to compensate by spoiling them with expensive clothes, gadgets and fancy holidays, but no amount of money can take the place of a parent.

## True Success: The Olive Tree.

> *"Your wife will be like a fruitful grapevine, flourishing within your home, Your children will be like vigorous young olive trees as they sit around your table."*
> **Psalm 128:3 NLT**

What does this mean? Why would the Bible use the Olive tree to describe our children? I did some research on this very profound Bible verse and what I discovered is very profound.

The Olive tree is a very fruitful tree. It can live for up to two thousand years. Some of the Olive trees that exist today are about two thousand years old. The trunks of these trees can grow to diameters of over two meters.

As the Olive tree gets older, the wood in the middle eventually disintegrates. This leaves the tree hollow, fragile and vulnerable to damage – especially damage as a result of high winds.

The amazing thing I found about the Olive Tree is that, to ensure its own safety, it will send up new shoots from its roots. Basically, as the tree grows older, new shoots (small young trees) begin to grow from the roots at the bottom. These shoots surround the "parent" tree and act as windbreaks. These windbreaks protect the fragile parent tree that is in the centre, and one of these shoots eventually takes up the position of the parent tree. [14]

> *"This provides a graphic illustration of the psalmist's vision of children who surround and support their aged, righteous parents. If we've done a good job as parents and as adult children, caring for our own parents when they need us, we can expect our children to follow the example that we (and the olive tree) have set for them, caring for us in our later years. It*

---

[14] "In situations where extreme cold has damaged or killed the olive tree the rootstock can survive and produce new shoots which in turn become new trees. In this way olive trees can regenerate themselves.

In Tuscany in 1985 a very severe frost destroyed many productive, and aged, olive trees and ruined many farmers' livelihoods. However new shoots appeared in the spring and, once the dead wood was removed, became the basis for new fruit-producing trees. In this way an olive tree can live for centuries or even millennia."

"Olive: Growth and propagation" Wikipedia. Retrieved January 22, 2017, from https://en.wikipedia.org/wiki/Olive

*is also a reminder of our obligations to our own parents and to our Heavenly Father."*
### Culled from torahflora.org

This is so profound.

*"In situations where extreme cold has damaged or killed the olive tree the rootstock can survive and produce new shoots which in turn become new trees. In this way olive trees can regenerate themselves. In Tuscany in 1985 a very severe frost destroyed many productive, and aged, olive trees and ruined many farmers' livelihoods. However new shoots appeared in the spring and, once the dead wood was removed, became the basis for new fruit-producing trees. In this way an olive tree can live for centuries or even millennia."*[15]

Remember the story of Noah? It was an Olive branch that the bird brought back as a sign of life. This means that the Olive tree survived the great flood and was possibly the only surviving tree. It could also mean that the Olive tree began to produce new shoots immediately after the great flood. The point here is that the Olive tree is able to survive great calamities.

---

[15] "This provides a graphic illustration of the psalmist's vision of children who surround and support their aged, righteous parents. If we've done a good job as parents and as adult children, caring for our own parents when they need us, we can expect our children to follow the example that we (and the olive tree) have set for them, caring for us in our later years. It is also a reminder of our obligations to our own parents and to our Heavenly Father."

Greenberg, Jon. "May your children be like olive trees." Torah Flora. Retrieved January 22, 2017, from http://www.torahflora.org/2008/08/may-your-children-be-like-olive-trees/

Like the Olive tree, children are meant to take care of parents in their old age. Children are meant to carry on the family name and vision.

> *Train up a child in the way He should go and*
> *when He is old, He would not depart from it.*
> **Proverbs 22:6 NKJV**

God is a generational God. He is interested in your generations to come, and He plans for generations. A generation is meant to outperform the previous generation, just look at Abraham and Isaac, Jacob and Joseph or David and Solomon. Children are meant to accomplish the things that their parents couldn't do in their own time. This is true wealth. But in order for this to happen, parents need to invest time and love in bringing up their children.

Unfortunately, most people neglect their children in the pursuit of money. Most of today's kids get infected by this new disease called Affluenza.[16] Their parents' pursuit of affluence leads to character deficiencies that they then spend time, energy and money trying to treat in their old age.

I met an American family sometime ago and, at the age of eighteen, the son had made his first million dollars. His father was a millionaire, as was his father before him. This was three generations of wealth. The last time I heard from them, the father was going to build hospitals in Namibia and his son was accompanying him. In sharp contrast, for many

---

[16] A psychological malaise supposedly affecting young wealthy people, symptoms of which include a lack of motivation, feelings of guilt, and a sense of isolation. The term "affluenza" has also been used to refer to an inability to understand the consequences of one's actions because of financial privilege.

"Affluenza." Wikipedia. Retrieved January 30, 2017, from https://en.wikipedia.org/wiki/Affluenza

families in Africa, it is common for wealth to be diminished in one generation.

## Ensuring Your Child's Success

So, how do you ensure your children become like Olive shoots round about your table? By spending time with your most precious gifts, by taking out time to nurture them, develop them, and groom them, and by spending time praying for them.

I use the book, *The Power Of A Praying Parent* by Stormie Omartian with regard to praying for my kids. It is such an amazing book and, similar to The Power of a Praying Wife, it has chapters for every day of the month. I have used this book over and over again for my children.

Prayer points include: becoming a praying parent, releasing my child into God's hands, securing protection from harm, feeling loved and accepted, establishing an eternal future, honouring parents and resisting rebellion, attracting godly friends and role models, and identifying God-given gifts and talents and even praying for your adult children. The prayers of a mother cannot be over emphasized.

It is also important to spend time reading the Word with your kids and teaching them how to pray. From when my children were very young, I tried as much as possible to spend time reading the Bible with them every evening. I have used different age-appropriate Bibles to make it easy for them to understand, and right now we are using Psalty's Kids Bible.

My daughters also love the book, *How To Be God's Little Princess - Royal Tips For Manners, Etiquette And True Beauty*, by Sheila Walsh. It is a wonderful way to teach them about God in a fun way, and also to build their character. At some point we used a devotional that was just for girls. We also use One Year Devotions for Pre-schoolers 2, by Crystal Bowman. Another really good online daily devotional is keysforkids.org.

After we read a devotional or Bible passage, I ask them to explain what they learnt, and we discuss it. Sometimes I give them tasks to practice what they learnt. For example, show kindness to two people at school tomorrow.

So many times, the Holy Spirit has used our devotion to speak to them or to make a point clear to my kids on my behalf. There was a day my daughters were fighting and by God incidence, the devotion of the day was referring to "inner beauty" i.e. character, and it had a graphic illustration of two girls fighting. That helped them learn that fighting isn't a sign of good character.

As soon as my older kids could talk, I allowed them to pray with us. Sometimes all they could say was, "God bless mummy, God bless daddy," but as they grew older, their prayers developed. Now that they're older – ten and seven – they take turns in leading us in our devotional time every evening. My son, who is about to turn two, joins us, too! He says "Amen" when he hears us say, "In Jesus' name," and He says, "Hallelujah" when we say, "Praise the Lord." He is aware that we have our prayer time and sometimes, if we are kneeling, he'll kneel with us. Once, I taught them a verse of Psalm 23 every morning on the way to school for a week, and they learnt the whole chapter.

When they want things I ask them to include it in their prayers. My older children prayed fervently for a baby brother. In fact, when I had let go and stopped praying about it, my daughters continued to pray. When God answered our prayers, they understood the importance of prayer and they knew it was God who did it.

It is important to be real with your kids, and not to paint a perfect picture of a world that isn't perfect. Be open with them about your struggles. One summer, we couldn't afford to travel on holiday and my daughter had been praying for a family holiday. I asked her to pray about it and she prayed every evening. One day, a friend of mine called to say that she was going away with her son for the summer, and she would love to take my daughter with her.

I was happy because God had answered her prayer, however, my daughter was reluctant because what she'd prayed for was a family holiday, and she didn't want to go on her own.

Then, the weekend before they were supposed to go, my friend called to say she hadn't been able to get a visa for my daughter. She felt bad about it, so she had made arrangements for my family to go on holiday! My husband agreed to the arrangement and we had one of the best holidays we've ever had. From this, my daughter has learnt that prayer and faith works. She has seen the power of prayer.

Playing with your children is so important. You can learn so much from play and recreation. My girls don't watch television during the week, so we have a movie night every Friday as a family. I also love our family holidays because it is just us, we get to do everything together without house helps or distractions.

In this walk of purpose, I find that I am getting even busier. When you do what you love, it's hard to draw the lines, so I have to be extra careful and intentional about spending time with my kids.

It is also possible to be physically there with your children but absent emotionally, especially in this age of social media. We must draw boundaries and do everything in moderation. It is not easy but thank God for the Holy Spirit who is our helper.

Your job as a parent is the third-most important job you will ever perform. It is second only to being a spouse and, of course, being the Father's daughter. The returns you will receive from the investment of your time in your children are to infinity.

You won't give your precious diamonds to unqualified people to keep for you, so why would you entrust someone else with your children?

Here are a few tips to ensuring your kids grow up to be all that God created them to be:

1. Pray, pray, pray. We can only achieve this through God's Grace.
2. Spend time with them.
3. Read the Bible with them.
4. Pray with them. Let them live your faith and not just hear it.
5. Discuss things of God with them.
6. Let them Experience God.
7. Teach them values.
8. Teach them the value of hard work.
9. Teach them the value of contentment.
10. Teach them to love others.
11. Teach them to be selfless.
12. Play with your children. You can learn a lot about the character of a child during playtime.
13. Pick them up from school and drop them off at school.
14. Teach them about money.
15. Encourage your children to ask questions.
16. Ask your children questions.
17. Invest in your children.

This list is not exhaustive. They are just tips and guides from research I've done, books I've read and also people I'm currently learning from. For example, I have a parenting mentor. In my first session with her, she said to me, "Parenting is a lonely walk." Not everyone will agree with your style, but it's okay.

A good book to read is *Experiencing God At Home*, by Tom and Richard Blackaby. It is a book on parenting God's way. You find that ministers of God – or even great men of God in the Bible – often failed at parenting. The Blackaby's are more than three generations of one family who are walking in the way of the Lord.

If you don't have children of your own yet, the Lord will bless you. The Lord is the one who gives.

I also want you to think of the Prophet Eli. His sons did not have good character but all was not lost, God caused Hannah to give him Samuel. Eli invested in Samuel and Samuel became one of the greatest prophets in Israel.

Samuel was his succession plan, and not his own biological children. There are many children who need Elis to bring out the best in them. They are waiting to be a part of the success story of your generation.

Most importantly, everything is by the Grace of God. We must pray and continue to depend on the Holy Spirit.

May our children be like Olive trees around our table in Jesus' name, Amen.

It is our duty as mothers to train up our children in the way they should go so that when they are old they won't depart from it. If we do this job well with God's grace, then like the Proverbs 31 woman, our children will rise up and call us blessed.

Parenting is a lot harder now, particularly with technology and social media. In the past, we tried to protect our kids from predators coming into our home, but now, these predators have easy access to attack under the guise of technology. Our children will face temptations, pressures, bullying in ways we would never have dreamed of. Some of the statistics are alarming:

- The largest consumer of Internet pornography is the twelve to seventeen age group.
- The average age of first Internet exposure to pornography is eleven years old.
- Seventy percent of sexual advances over the Internet happened while youngsters were on the computer. [17]

As parents, we must be watchful; I have heard of female house helps molesting children of either gender, in addition to the stories of male molesters.

I also implore you to monitor your kids during visits and sleepovers. I remember sleeping over at a childhood friend's house when I was a young child. She had been exposed to pornography and she kissed me a few times. When I went to secondary school and became aware of the concept of lesbianism, I thought I could be a lesbian. I soon realised it was based on what happened as a child.

We must also educate our children about these issues; I have regular sexual awareness talks with my daughters.

The work we have to do as parents is enormous. We can't afford to sleep on duty; we must be vigilant and attentive; we must always cover our children in prayer.

We must involve the Holy Spirit in our parenting journey. As we watch and pray, He will guide us.

---

[17] From Experiencing God at Home, by Tom and Richard Blackaby.

Does this mean we have to compromise our careers in order to be good mothers? No, I don't believe so. I believe that the key thing is walking in purpose.

God knows the purpose He created you for and, in that purpose, He will make it possible for you to do all. Yes, you may have to make some sacrifices, but all sacrifices pay off; it's all about knowing the times and seasons.

For instance, I know that I'm called to be an international speaker. However, at this point in my life, I also know that I can't just go all over the world while I'm raising my kids. So, for my international speaking trips, I will have to prayerfully work it around my kids' schedules. I may decide to schedule my foreign trips during their school holidays or decide to take time out and make up for it – it's all about being intentional in making it work.

Having a supportive husband is also very important. Studies show that children with paternal involvement have higher levels of psychological well-being and better cognitive abilities than those without.[18] I am grateful for a supportive husband who would gladly fill the vacuum if God says it's time to travel the world.

That said, it is important to put career in its rightful place: after your role as the Father's daughter, after your role as a wife, and after your role as a mother.

---

[18] "Studies from around the world have concluded that children benefit greatly from paternal involvement. Research over the last 40 years has consistently found that in comparison to children with less-involved fathers, children with involved and loving fathers have higher levels of psychological well-being and better cognitive abilities. When fathers provide even just routine childcare, children have higher levels of educational and economic achievement and lower delinquency rates. These children even tend to be more empathetic and socially competent. These findings are true for children from all socio-economic back grounds, whether or not the mother is highly involved."

-Sheryl Sandberg, From *Lean In*.

I currently work from home. I start work when my kids are at school and I pick them up when they are done with school. This way, I work my schedule around my kids and not the other way round. It still isn't the easiest and I sometimes compromise, but the difference is that I am aware of the importance of my role, and I try to adjust my schedules and routines to make up for lost time. I know what I could have been earning if I was still working in my previous career, but I have decided to sacrifice that in order to give my kids the best of my time.

The beauty about working in purpose is that my career is not suffering. God has taken me to heights that only He can, and He has opened doors for me that no one else could have. He has put me in a place of influence in such a short period of time, a place that would have taken me decades to achieve in my previous career, if I even ever reached it.

I have won awards, been listed as one of the most influential women in Nigeria, spoken amongst some of the greatest leaders and dignitaries in Nigeria and even internationally. I have hosted events at some of the most expensive venues in Nigeria, I have appeared in, and been interviewed by, some of the most prestigious publications in Nigeria, Africa and internationally. I have impacted hundreds of people through my events and thousands of people through my social media platforms, and I do all this from the comfort of my home. I am able to soar in my career and also work at being the best wife and mother.

I am able to live the Richer life.

# Components of the Richer Woman

Once the Richer Woman understands her roles as the Father's Daughter, as a wife and as a mother, she will come into an understanding of her purpose.

That's the first step.

After that, there are components of her life that must be taken care of in order to make the journey smooth.

Consider this analogy: If you have to ride a car to a destination, you'll get there faster if the wheels of the car are well rounded and balanced. However, if your wheels aren't round – if they have edges or are punctured – you may never even get to your destination.

The wheels represent your life. Choosing to live the richer life by becoming "The Richer Woman" is like choosing to use the well-rounded and well-balanced wheels in the journey of life.

There's a life-coaching tool called the wheel of life. It helps ensure you are balanced and fulfilled in all areas of your life.

The Richer Woman's "wheel of life" consists of the following component parts:

1. Spirituality
2. Family
3. Work/Career/Achievements
4. Health and Wellbeing
5. Friendships/Relationships
6. Fun/Recreation/Rest
7. Money and Finances
8. Time

Let's look at each one individually.

# Spirituality

*"For everything, absolutely everything, above and below, visible and invisible... everything got started in Him and finds its purpose in Him."*

**– Colossians 1:16 (MSG)**

Everything begins with and ends with God. The world is changing and a lot of people are depressed because they have no faith or hope in God. Life has failed them. All that man has put his hopes on is crumbling. The only thing that is constant is God.

If you lay the right foundation, then all other areas of your life will be fine. Like a house: the deeper and stronger the foundation, the higher the house can go.

As I'm writing this book, my youngest daughter has been asked to have surgery. This morning, as I got up to write, my oldest daughter complained of pain in her knee and lower leg, and I am going to take her to the hospital. I spent some time with God and the word He gave me was, *"Be strong and courageous, do not be afraid or dismayed, for the Lord your God is with you wherever you go."* (**Joshua 1:9**). His word gave me peace.

*In the world you will have tribulation; but be of good cheer, I have overcome the world.*

**John 16:3 NKJV**

We will always go through trials. Giving your life to Jesus or being a Christian does not mean you will have a problem-free life. In fact, you will be attacked even more because you are a child of God. The beautiful thing is that, like the bible says in **Joshua** Chapter **1 verse 9**, God says He will be with us.

Whether or not you're a Christian, you will go through challenges. I'd rather go through those challenges with God on my side.

## Investing in Our Relationship with God:

As with all things in life, we must spend time developing and building our relationship with God. We spend huge amounts of money and time going for degrees, masters programs, courses, seminars and conferences, and we also need to invest into developing our relationship with God.

The game-changer for me has been the discipleship classes I took at my church, Guiding Light Assembly. There are three courses: Masterlife, Experiencing God and Mind of Christ.

Masterlife helps you with putting Jesus at the centre of your life, becoming more like Him even in character, helps with prayer, and discovering your purpose, gifts and ministry. Experiencing God helps you develop a deep intimate relationship with God and Mind of Christ helps you develop the mind of Christ by the help of the Holy Spirit. It doesn't matter how long you have been a Christian; there are people who have been Christians for over decades, who have done the discipleship courses and testify to their lives being changed. It is free and you don't have to be a member of Guiding Light Assembly to sign up for the classes. Please follow Guiding Light Assembly on Facebook, Twitter and

Instagram for more details @guidinglightGLA @ignitegla. There are Masterlife discipleship classes available in other parts of the world.

Wherever you are in the world, take out time to develop your relationship with God. Your local church or even other churches in your city may have a bible study, cell groups or discipleship classes you can join.

## Prayer:

It is also important to spend quiet time with God, praying daily. Spend time just sitting in His presence, basking in His love and worshipping Him. Our relationship with God is a two-way relationship; He also wants to talk to us! It is important to spend time not saying anything, but just listening. It is also important to read your Bible, meditate on it and also study it. You can also use a devotional, but you must grow to the point where you can read the word yourself and hear from God. Masterlife helps with this.

Prayer is also very important. You can use prayer books. I particularly love Stormie Omartian's books: The Power of a Praying Wife and The Power of a Praying Parent. They help me pray for my husband and children. I also like Pastor Goke Coker's book, Godfessions, it helps me speak God's words and promises into my life, future and the atmosphere. I also declare and read certain Psalms out loud, depending on what I'm facing.

Your words have creative power. I don't spend that much time on prayers that require taking your eyes off Jesus and focusing on the devil. Jesus already won the victory. The battle is the Lord's. When you are in His will and walking in purpose, there is protection. The key thing is ensuring that you stay in a place of obedience. John Maxwell, in his

Leadership Bible, puts it well. He says, "There are different stages of spiritual maturity. The issues for 'little children' are getting right with God and forgiven sins. For 'young men' it is waging spiritual warfare and defeating opposition while for fathers, it is intimacy with God. Our goal should be to grow to the 'father' stage and have intimacy with God."

Prayer doesn't have to be so complicated or formal. When you talk to your earthly father, spouse or your friends, you just talk, right? No unnecessary ceremony. This is the way it should be with your Heavenly Father. I talk to God like I'm talking to my Father or friend. You don't have to be formal. I try to remember to talk to Him all through the day, when I'm doing regular tasks like driving. You can even talk to Him while you are in the toilet.

He doesn't want the conversation to end with quiet time. Quiet time gives you a place with no distractions so you can be completely focused on Him, hear from Him and just be with Him, just you and Him, but He also wants to go with you as you carry out your activities for the day. He is with you and in you.

I also love to write in my journal, it is like writing a letter or an email to God.

## Fasting:

Taking out time to fast is important. Now, fasting is not denying yourself of food and staying hungry so that God can be moved to do something in your life – God is God and He has already completed everything He has begun. Fasting is denying your flesh so that you can feed your spirit. It is removing all distractions so that you can hear God and be alert in the spirit. There are also many different ways you can fast. Never ever follow any crowd. You must always be led by the Holy Spirit. In 2016, I was led by the Holy Spirit to do the Daniel fast and it was phenomenal. You can also take time away from social media so that you can move away from noise and distractions. Fasting should not only be done ceremoniously, we must live the fasted life.

## Spending Time with God:

Several times in the Bible, we're told that Jesus moved away from the crowd to pray by Himself. We must be like Jesus and do this as often as possible.

Once in a while, you can even go on a retreat to a different location just to spend time with God.

In 2013, just after I resigned, I went on a two-day trip to Ghana with one of my close friends. We went on Friday morning and returned on Sunday evening. I called it "The Lady and Her Lord." We prayed together in the morning, went our separate ways during the day and returned to spend time together at dinner. It was such an amazing time of refreshing and rest. It was one of my favourite holidays ever because I got to spend quality time with God.

## Fellowship with Believers:

It is important for me to try to go to church every Sunday, fellowship with believers is so important. We are a body and we need each other to function. When one is weak, the other is strong.

Being active in your church is also important. You may feel distant in your church but if you give your time, you will form relationships in return. I sought this in 2012 when I joined the MasterLife course and I formed life-long relationships. I also taught MasterLife and served in church.

Every Monday, my prayer partner and I meet to pray together. It has become a time of fellowship and sharing. So many times we have celebrated each other, we have worshipped God, and received answers to our prayers. Other times we have cried and been in despair, but where one is weak the other is strong and encourages the other. I'm not sure how I would have passed through some of the tests I went through in my marriage without the support, prayers and encouragement of my prayer partner. We have formed a life-long relationship that has blossomed.

I love going for faith inspired events, most especially worship events like the Night of Worship and T.H.U.G (This House Under God). For me, I love every opportunity to just worship and praise God.

## Guarding Our Hearts:

I also try to protect my mind and spirit man as much as possible with the kind of music I listen to or television programs or movies I watch. As you grow in your relationship with God, you will not even have to force these things. You put off the old and put on the new. Trust me, I used to love going clubbing and partying. Today, I don't remember the last time I went to a club. It's not because I was forced to, or feel it is an obligation as a Christian. It's because I just don't see the point any longer. I'd rather spend the time at home sleeping or, better still, praying.

My husband loves music. His collection of music is unbelievable. As I grew in my walk with Christ and began to listen to more life and spirit building music, I was concerned about some of the music my husband listened to. I would be listening to praise and worship upstairs and hip-hop would be playing downstairs. Today, my husband's Christian collection is unbelievable. In fact, I learn about the latest worship songs or albums from him. God is so faithful. Like Joyce Meyer says, one thing she has learnt in 50 years of marriage is that you can't change anyone. Only God can do the changing. You focus on doing your own part.

## Other Resources:

I also read a lot of Christian books, blog posts and watch and listen to sermons on YouTube by Christian leaders that I follow. A few of my favourites are Joyce Meyer, Steven Furtick, Sarah Jakes Roberts and Priscilla Shirer. Right now, I'm reading a couple of books at the same time: Driven by Eternity by John Bevere, and I hope to finish reading Experiencing God at Home by Tom and Richard Blackaby this year.

## Spirituality and Family:

It is also important to carry your family along in your relationship with God. Men are supposed to be the Priest of the home, the spiritual leaders, but many women have taken up this role. It is important to ensure that we pray our husbands into taking up their rightful positions as the spiritual leaders of the home.

Here's an analogy that was shared with me: While God was making Eve, Adam was asleep. When He finished, He woke Adam up. Sometimes, God works on the relationship with the wives first. This could be because once the husband catches the fire or the vision, he'll run with it. Many women can testify that once their husbands grew in their relationships with Christ they took it to a whole new level. My husband's depth is on a whole different level. Sometimes I'm like, "Dude, chill, now!"

There should be daily prayer between husband and wife and there should also be prayer and devotional time with the whole family.

## Summary

**The Richer Woman knows that without God she can do nothing. She knows that her relationship with God is her most prized asset. She seeks God diligently and focuses on improving her relationship with Him. She is aware that once she has God, all other things will fall into place.**

## Action Points

a. Score your relationship with God on a scale of 1-10.
b. Why did you rate yourself this way?
c. List five things you are going to do differently to ensure you develop and improve your relationship with God. Include dates you intend to achieve these five things.
d. List five things you will stop doing to ensure your relationship with God grows. Include dates you intend to stop these five things.

# Family

*"Family is not an important thing, it is everything."*
**Michael J Fox.**

Beyond everything I've shared on the roles of a woman as a wife and a mother, family also consists of the extended family: parents, siblings, in-laws. You must make out time for all the relationships that God brings your way, especially the God-ordained ones like family. I believe He will hold us accountable for all our relationships.

I am working on this. I need to make out more time to spend with my parents, siblings and in-laws. It is really difficult, especially with my schedule, but as with all things it is all about planning and being intentional. One way I plan to tackle this in my own life is by creating a schedule to plan my time, so that I can create time for other members of our family.

We must also nurture our relationships with our spouses. We must spend time alone with them. Date night, movie night and holidays for just the two of you.

We must also do the same with our kids. Family time together is also important, and it's important to take family vacations to locations where you don't have too many distractions, such as people to visit. One of my favourite trips was our trip to Dubai in 2016. We really bonded as a family.

Even if you can't afford to travel to a place like Dubai, you can go to African countries if you are based in Africa, or go to holiday spots in close proximity to your country or city. One of my favourite holidays was our trip as a family to Kenya. It was so beautiful. I know of a family who took a road trip to Ghana with their kids. You can go to Cotonou, and there are even really nice locations in Nigeria. My husband and I recently attended a wedding at La Campagne Tropicana beach resort. We stayed the night and it was really nice.

Dream big and start small. One day I hope to visit Australia to go and worship at Hillsong.

In my family, we also have movie night every Friday as a family. One way we are encouraging our children to walk in the faith is by watching faith-based movies with them. We have watched Heaven is For Real, Miracles from Heaven, War Room and God is not Dead together as a family. I watch movies with my husband on Sunday nights since I don't work on Mondays.

As the Richer Women, we are also responsible for our family's overall wellbeing, just like the Proverbs 31 woman. Our husband and kids must eat healthy, sleep well, and we need to cover them with prayer. We cannot outsource our responsibilities to domestic staff.

God has blessed us with all we need. Women are great at multitasking and I believe this is because of the various hats we wear. Thankfully, we don't have to do it alone. We have the Holy Spirit, who is our helper. We must rely on His strength.

I believe God will ask what we did with what He gave us; we have a lot of work to do.

## Summary

The Richer Woman knows that family is dear to God's heart. She doesn't neglect her family in pursuit of her own goals and ambition. She is aware that God has put her in her family for a purpose. She is aware that her role in her family is the second most important role she would ever perform, more important than any awards, accolades, titles or achievements.

## Action Points

a. Score your relationship with your family or your role as a member of your family on a scale of 1-10.
b. Why did you rate yourself this way?
c. List five things you will do differently to ensure you improve on your role and relationship in your family. Include dates you intend to achieve these five things.
d. List five things you will stop doing to ensure your relationship with your family improves. Include dates you intend to stop these five things.

# Work/Career/Achievements

*"Work with purpose."*
**Anonymous**

This component is very important for most women. Due to my childhood experiences, I always wanted to be a very successful career woman. I wanted to be Minister of Finance and the World Bank President. I had very big dreams, but my perspective has changed due to my life experiences.

Life is fleeting; you are here today and gone tomorrow. What is the point of all these achievements if they are not part of your purpose?

I have gone from a career-driven woman to a woman driven by purpose. Whatever you are doing must be aligned with purpose and must bring God glory.

At the same time, it is important to note that there is no right or wrong career; God needs people in different spheres to do His work. He needs doctors, accountants, lawyers, engineers, entrepreneurs, actors, musicians and homemakers (yes, it is a job and can be a full-time one, too). He is the author of work and I believe He requires us to work – note that I didn't say, "get a job". That's because His idea of what work might be different from our idea. He wants us to succeed in whatever form of work we engage in.

The problem, though, is when we work in an area where we were not called to work. This occurs mainly because of the pursuit of money, security, prestige and such things. I wanted to be an investment banker because I wanted to be rich, but this was not God's purpose for me.

The world will tell you to dream big, set goals and you'll be a success. I did have big dreams but they were not God's dreams for me.

I remember an analogy I heard once. Imagine climbing up a very tall building, getting to the top and realising that you are on the wrong building. Many people will get to the end of their career and life and realise they are on the wrong building. Many people plan to begin to do what they were called to do when they are older or when they retire, but time is not guaranteed to anyone.

God created us all uniquely and blessed us with many gifts. We are all talented. Sometimes, we don't even know how talented we are and we have to dig deep. Sometimes, God will even use our weaknesses as if they were strengths.

All I ever wanted to do was work in finance and I was blinded to the gifts God had deposited in me. I thank God that I decided to stop following my own dreams and I began to seek His will and purpose for my life.

How do you know the purpose of a thing? You have to ask its creator. That's what I did.

One day, I went to a toastmasters events and I met a US diplomat. She asked me what I did and I said I used to be in investment banking. She said she had a gift for helping people discover their purpose, and that I looked like I should be in media. I thought, media? It had never even occurred to me. By God incidence, when my Pastor asked me to volunteer at Church, the role that was available was in media and I went on to become the Head of Media and Publications at Guiding Light Assembly. Today I am a co-host on a talk show that airs in forty-four African countries and the UK and is watched all over the world on YouTube.

I'm not just a life coach, I am also a motivational speaker. I remember when I told my colleagues at the investment banking company I worked in that I had resigned and I wasn't sure what I was going to do next. One of my colleagues said, "You should be a motivational speaker."

I was afraid to leave my job but, today, the same challenges I faced is what I now use to encourage others to walk in purpose through "Do It Afraid." The "Do It Afraid" mantra has impacted so many lives.

My career in personal finance also started in the most unexpected way.

One particular Monday, I had spent most of my day with God. When I was done, I saw that I had missed a call from an acquaintance. She asked what I did and I said I wasn't doing anything but I used to work in finance. She said she had recommended me and four other people to the editor of a lifestyle magazine who was looking for someone to host a personal finance column. Without knowing me, or what I do, the editor chose me. I called her and she asked me to send her two articles. At this point I didn't even know I could write, but I remembered that when I was leaving my old place of work, I had written a farewell email that got everyone emotional. One of my colleagues said to me, "Omi, you have a gift in writing, explore it."

When this opportunity came, I called that colleague and said, "Your prophecy has come to pass. I don't know what to do."

He said, "You can do it. Just write about that Prada bag or savings plan."

That's how my career in personal finance started.

Amazingly, the things I teach are based on the lessons I learnt in my pursuit of money, even though my previous role was corporate finance and not personal finance.

I am in complete awe of some of the opportunities God has brought my way. Truly, His words don't lie when He says, *"Now to Him who is able to do exceedingly abundantly above all that we ask or think, according to the power that works in us."* **(Ephesians 3:20 NKJV)**

> *"Eye has not seen nor ear heard, nor have entered into the heart of man, the things which God has prepared for those who love Him."*
> **1 Corinthians 2:9 MEV**

God has already exceeded my expectations beyond my wildest imagination and the beautiful thing about it is that this is only the beginning. I'm so thankful that I chose to walk in His purpose for me.

I've also come to realize that God has different plans for His daughters. Like me, some people may be required to work from home. I love working from home and thank God for technology as I can reach the world from the comfort of my home. I also get to be a better wife and mother. I feel like I'm eating my cake and having it at the same time.

For some, God may say His plan is for you to be a homemaker and to support your husband's vision. Don't feel bad if you are one of those and don't feel pressure to be what He hasn't called you to be. God's plans are always sovereign.

I know someone who tried to get a job several times but couldn't, and whenever she tried to do business it didn't work. She realized that God's plans for her were different. Today, she is responsible for the growth of many people's relationships with God, including mine. She has discipled so many people, and God has blessed her husband tremendously. In my opinion, she is very successful. She is living the Richer life.

Perhaps your purpose may be to bring up your children in the way of the Lord so that they can be used by God effectively for His kingdom, don't compare yourself to others who are called to be in the marketplace. The key thing is walking in purpose; doing that thing that God created you to do.

God is not going to reward you on the titles you have gained or obtained but on what He asked you to do. I've come across many women who are depressed because they feel they haven't achieved much at their age. Most of these women are comparing themselves to social media personalities and this is so wrong. Life is not a competition; we were all made differently. We all have our own race to run.

Some women are called to work in professional careers, however this should not be at the expense of their families. You have to be intentional about it and ensure you have the right systems in place. You must not outsource your responsibility as a wife or mother to third parties. Yes, nannies and domestic staff are necessary, but remember that they are just helps and should not take our place as parents.

I met a lady who shared her own experience with me. Due to the fact that her husband was travelling a lot, she took some time off from her career so she could be the best wife to her husband and mother to her children but she made sure that she kept developing herself. During that period she completed her Masters degree. Eventually, when her kids had grown up, she took on a role as Chief Financial Officer of a large organization.

Her last child was 7 when she took up the role, and so she would drop him at school and go to work and close from work around the same time he finished from school so she could be with him at home.

I also believe that, for women who God has called to pursue time-consuming careers, He blesses them with supportive spouses who will have more time for the kids. This is perfectly fine. The problem only arises when both parents are unavailable.

If you are a single mother, you need a strong support system that may consist of family and friends. You are not alone. You have the Holy Spirit as your helper. You can prayerfully seek father figures within your network that could form a relationship with your child, but please do this prayerfully, and make sure you don't leave your child without supervision, as there are a lot of predators out there. If your child's father is alive, please encourage a relationship between your child and his/her father as much as it is possible.

There will come a time when your kids are of a certain age; when you have instilled all those values in them and you can soar in all areas of your life. It is said that the crucial point of a child's life is age 0-10. Once you have done your bit, the world is your oyster. You wouldn't want to spend the time you could use to soar in your life and career to run from one rehab centre to the other.

God often gives us different assignments for different seasons. Sometimes, we are required to take advantage of the low hanging fruits while you keep your eye on the big fruit at the top.

The key thing is to trust Him and be obedient to what He tells you to do. The assignments change, but the vision stays the same. Our mantra should be to follow **Matthew Chapter 6 verse 33,** which says, *"But Seek ye first the Kingdom of God and His righteousness and all things would be added unto us."*

When it comes to purpose, God reveals the big picture but He doesn't reveal all the steps to getting there; He takes it one step at a time. I believe He does this intentionally because, if He were to give us the all the steps and the journey we are to take, we would run with it and leave Him behind! Other times, if He were to reveal all the steps at once, the magnitude of His plans could overwhelm us.

By revealing each step at a time, we learn to come back to Him each time for direction. We learn to depend on Him and trust Him. This way we establish a **relationship** with Him, which is God's desire for all His children.

Having a relationship with God is the key thing to discovering your purpose. Spend time with Him. Pray to Him to reveal your purpose and He will begin to open doors. Things will begin to align and work in your favour.

The world tells us to look to our talents and passion as indicators of our purpose, but I don't agree. For example, I was shy and never would have imagined that I would be a motivational speaker. God knew this and along the process, He ensured I developed my gift. I would also never have imagined that I would have had a career in media. Truly, He uses the foolish things of the world to confound the wise.

Recently, someone shared a word from God that said, "God will begin to magnify our weaknesses as though they were strengths," and it is already evident. I know a lady who is the leading special effects and lighting specialist in Nigeria. She studied linguistics in school and never would have imagined that she would be in such a technical industry.

When He gives you a vision, write it down, it shall not tarry.

*Then the* Lord *answered me and said: "Write the vision And make it plain on tablets, That he may run who reads it. For the vision is yet for an appointed time; But at the end it will speak, and it will not lie. Though it tarries, wait for it; Because it will surely come, It will not tarry."*

**Habakkuk 2:2-3 (NKJV)**

Once you have discovered what you are called to do, the key thing is to develop your potential. I read a story on the process of preparation from Joyce Meyers' book, The Making of a Leader. It tells of:

*"A young man who found a treasure but didn't know how to access it, so he studied hard to learn how to cultivate his treasure. hands on, took every course on it he could find and talked to every person who would give him any information about it. He did nothing else for that entire year but learn about mining. He laid aside everything else in his life in order to devote his entire attention to learning how to mine gold.*

*At the end of the tedious preparation process, he reaped great rewards.* [19]*year, he went*

---

[19] "A young man found a vein of gold in a mountain. He tried to get it out himself but kept failing repeatedly. He felt like giving up, but instead he went into town and asked a mining agency to come take a look at it. The mining company surveyed the mountain and the vein of gold and wanted to buy it. They offered the young man a large amount of cash if he would sell it to them.

The young man thought about it and decided that rather than selling it to the mining company, he would keep it and learn all he could about mining. Over the next year he studied practically day and night. He read every book on mining he could lay his hands on, took every course on it he could find and talked to every person who would give him any information about it. He did nothing else for that entire year but learn about mining. He laid aside everything else in his life in order to devote his entire attention to learning how to mine gold.

> *back to the mountain and began to dig out the gold, it was tremendously hard work, but in the end he had millions and millions of dollars."*

What do you have in your hand? Develop it. There is a place for preparation. There is a place for developing our gifts and talents. We have to prepare for the place of purpose.

Jesus didn't start His ministry until He was 30 years old. He spent the first thirty years preparing for a role that would only last for three years on this earth. What He was really preparing for was eternity.

Do not despise the time of preparation. If you are not prepared for a place of purpose you will likely fail when you get to that place. There is a reason why we're not born adults. We start of as babies, then become toddlers, girls, teenagers, ladies and then women. We spend a lot of time preparing for the time we will be women and then, when we are women, we give birth to babies and help them prepare as well.

There is a place for starting small. I did not become Africa's Premier Wealth coach overnight. After I graduated from school, I got a job in a post room at the London Borough of Camden. I would sit in the room myself, open mails and sort them out. I worked alone in that post room. I didn't know that God was preparing me for my current role. As I write this book, I work from home and I'm physically alone. I have people on my team, however they work virtually.

There is a process in everything and we mustn't circumvent the process. We must trust God in the process.

---

At the end of the year, he went back to the mountain and began to dig out the gold, it was tremendously hard work, but in the end he had millions and millions of dollars."

– Joyce Meyer. From *The Making of a Leader*.

## Summary

**The Richer Woman is a woman of purpose. She is not in a race or competition with anyone. She knows her unique calling and she is comfortable with it. Her goal in life is to fulfil God's purpose for her.**

## Action Points

a. Score yourself on a scale of 1-10 with regard to your work, career or achievements. Ask yourself the following questions:

Are you fulfilled? Are you walking in purpose? Do you enjoy the work you do? Does your work encroach on your other responsibilities?

b. Why did you rate yourself this way?
c. List five things that you are going to do differently to ensure you walk in purpose and are fulfilled. Include dates you intend to achieve these five things.
d. List five things you will stop doing, to ensure you are walking in purpose and are fulfilled. Include dates you intend to stop doing these five things.

# Health and Wellbeing

*"The greatest wealth is health."*
**Virgil**

Many women neglect their health. We get lost in our responsibilities as wives, mothers and career women and forget to take care of ourselves, but if we don't take care of ourselves we won't be able to be our best in our other roles.

This analogy may help us understand why it is so important to take care of ourselves: In case of an emergency on an airplane, the cabin crew insist that passengers must put on their oxygen masks firsts, before helping the next person – even if it is a child. If a mother doesn't have oxygen to breathe, she may not survive, and then she'll be useless to help anyone around her.

In the same way, you must help yourself and ensure you are in good health so that you are able to fulfil your other roles.

This is an area I'm struggling with and hope to improve on. Previously, I had a personal trainer and I used to involve myself in activities such a netball and water aerobics, but I haven't done these in a while. I also used to go for daily walks with my kids. My goal is to start small and begin walking again every evening with my kids. I would also like to include 15-minute workout sessions every morning. Once I have mastered these, the intention is to increase the pace of exercise. I also love swimming and would like to go swimming once a week with my kids.

Eating healthy is also a very important goal for me. I have a sweet tooth and I love chocolates and fizzy drinks. Going on the Daniel fast last year really helped me let go of some not-so-great eating habits. I no longer use milk. I use honey instead of sugar and I have cut down on my fizzy drinks.

I read this amazing book, Fight Stress & Live: 5 Simple Commitments That Can Save Your Life, by Genette Howard. The author says it's best to focus on eating as many whole foods as possible. Whole foods include sweet potatoes (yam), fruits, vegetables and whole grains (oats).

I need to eat more vegetables and fruit and include it in our family meals as well.

It is good to have all these wishes but it is more important to have goals. Goals are dreams with deadlines. Goals must be S.M.A.R.T: **S**pecific, **M**easurable, **A**chievable, **R**ealistic and **T**ime-bound.

I will ensure that my schedule includes SMART health and fitness goals.

Sometimes we can get discouraged and overwhelmed with all the new super foods we see on social media, and the heavy workouts people do, but we must pace ourselves, start small and focus on our own race.

Take out time to go to the spa. Pamper yourself. Treat yourself to something you really like. Buy that nice dress or that nice bag or shoes. Go for facials. Take care of your hair. Love yourself. Take yourself out for dinner. There is absolutely nothing wrong in going out to dinner by yourself. Enjoy your own company. Celebrate yourself. You will find that this will boost your self-esteem and confidence levels, and it will do a lot for your health and wellbeing. Remember to treat yourself like a princess and a Queen.

## *Summary*

**Despite her many roles, The Richer Woman doesn't forget to take care of herself. She is not lost in her various roles. She takes good care of herself and she is fit for purpose.**

## *Actions Points*

a. Score your health and wellbeing on a scale of 1-10.
b. Why did you rate yourself this way?
c. List five things you are going to begin to do differently to ensure you are in good health and you have high energy levels. Include dates you would like to achieve these things.
d. List five things you intend to stop doing to ensure you are in good health and you have high energy levels. Include dates you intend to stop doing these five things.

# Friendships/Relationships

*"True friendship is a gift - priceless gift from God. For women in particular, spending intimate time with friends is not a luxury but a necessity for healthy living."*
**Genette Howard.**

As women, it is important to have friends and to nurture our relationships. It is an essential part of our wellbeing. Sometimes, women neglect their friendships when they get married or have kids, however what they fail to realize is that every relationship has its own purpose. While your husband or kids can be your friends, you must also have friends separate from these relationships. In the past, women went to fetch water by the stream and they would use this opportunity to talk to the older women or their peers, to fill this role.

Men and women have different biochemistry. According to Genette Howard,[20] the hormone used to fight stress in men is testosterone while the stress-fighting hormone in women is oxytocin. Men replenish their testosterone by resting, while women release and replenish their oxytocin when they engage in nurturing activities. One

---

[20] From: *Fight Stress & Live - 5 Simple Commitments That Can Save Your Life*, by Genette Howard.

way this manifests in marriage is that women like to talk while men just want to relax. This is often the cause of many disagreements in marriage.

The key thing is to strike a balance. In the past, I used to complain that my husband never made time to talk to me. I thought I had made a mistake and married the wrong person. What I didn't realize is that most men need their lone time, in front of the TV, watching football or similar activities, to rest and replenish their hormones. Now I've found a formula that works. When my husband gets home from work, I give him time to rest alone and then afterwards I go to sit with him. Just resting on him helps me feel connected. We may decide to chat about our day but if we don't, it's fine. Being next to him feels wonderful. I learnt this from Genette Howards book.

My friendships with my girlfriends also help me in this regard. If I need to talk for long, I call or chat with my girlfriends. I've taken the pressure of my need to talk for long hours, off my husband.

As a woman, having friends is very important. I have been blessed with some of the most amazing friends. I have friends that I have known all my life and I also have new friends. Recently, my friends, soul sisters, and I, had a photo shoot to celebrate our friendship. I posted two of the photographs on social media and I was amazed at the response. Many female-based organisations reposted the pictures, but what was more alarming was the fact that I received messages from women saying that they wished they had this kind of relationship. I spoke to a particular lady who shared her loneliness, and said she hopes to make friends this year. Truly, true friendship is a priceless gift from God.

I also hear that a lot of women are wary of other women, but I have had a lot of good experiences. I do not take this for granted because I don't have any sisters, so my friends, cousins and in-laws are my sisters. I have had very few bad experiences in the past, but I count it all joy because I learn from every experience.

I have relationships with people of different ages. I have younger friends that I mentor who have become my friends, prayer partners and even confidants. I have older friends and cousins that I pray with and share some of my deepest concerns with.

In this walk of purpose, God has also brought the most amazing new friends my way. Our relationships are new but we are Kingdom sisters. God is connecting His daughters. They have been pillars of strength in this walk of purpose.

It's not the quantity that matters, but the quality, and I treasure each and every relationship dearly. They add colour to my life and have helped me through some of the toughest times in my life. God has used them in various ways to be a blessing to me. I believe they have been more of a blessing than I have been to and for them.

I believe friendships are food to the soul of a woman. It's nice to have someone to laugh with, cry with, share with, and pray with. I don't know how I would have coped during some of the challenges I've gone through – even my temptations – without my friends. The second time I had to travel with my mum for her surgery, it fell around my daughter's $5^{th}$ birthday and I couldn't be there. My friends and cousins came together to host a surprise birthday party for her in my absence. When I faced temptations in my marriage, my best friend, another friend, my cousin and my prayer partner, held me accountable and prayed with me.

I love the saying that goes, "If you're the smartest person in the class then you are in the wrong class." Your friends should inspire and motivate you and should either be growing at the same level, or be at higher growth levels than you.

A preacher came to minster at our church in 2014 and she said something very profound. She said, "In order to succeed, you must have a dream team. A dream team should consist of a mentor, a confidant, buddy, a coach, a sponsor and a Judas in your life." I'll add a Prayer Partner and mentees to the list.

A **mentor** is someone who has walked the path you would like to walk and you learn from this person. I have so many mentors. Some, I haven't met before, like Joyce Meyer, Terri Savelle Foy, John Maxwell and Heather Lindsey. You don't have to be in close proximity to your mentor. Thank God for technology, you can learn from any location. It is also good to have mentors in close proximity. My Pastor and my life coach are my mentors; they're like Fathers to me. My cousin is also my mentor.

I also have a parenting mentor. One day I was praying to God about my parenting style. Some people don't agree with my parenting style and I needed God to confirm that I was on the right track. I asked for a mentor and He led me to her. When we met up for the first time, we talked for quite a bit. We had so much in common and she encouraged me. She said to me, "Parenting is a lonely walk."

Coincidentally, she, too, left her job as an investment banker, to work as a University Lecturer. Today, she is the Special Adviser to the President, Office of the Vice-President of Nigeria.

It is important not to idolise mentors. The Holy Spirit is the ultimate mentor.

A **coach** is someone who believes in you, encourages you and keeps you accountable. I am a life-coach, but even a coach needs a coach, thus I also have a coach.

Some of the greatest leaders of our time, even some of the executives of some of the biggest corporations, have coaches. I also have clients who I have coaching relationships with. The wonderful thing about technology is that you don't have to be in the same location with me to be my coachee.

There's a difference between a confidant and a buddy, and it is important not to mix the two. A **buddy** should be kept strictly for that purpose. The minister shared that her husband had a friend he would play video games with for many years. When she asked his name or where he lived, her husband said he didn't know; all they did was play video games.

In choosing **confidants,** you have to be very discerning and careful. Sometimes the closest people to you are the ones who have access to hurting you. Pray about the people who are close to you and ask God to reveal every 'frenemy'. Ask for a spirit of discernment.

Do not surround yourself with people who don't have a vision or who do not exhibit the same values as you. Do not surround yourself with people who envy you and do not want you to excel. This is important, as the friends you have can make or mar your destiny.

During the tough years of my marriage, my cousin and my best friend would always encourage me with good advice. They never said anything bad about my husband or take my side; neither did they encourage me to leave my marriage. They would always make me see my husband's point of view or God's point of view. You need people like this around you.

People say you shouldn't share your marital problems and, while some of the reasons might be valid, this has also led to many women going into depression or making the wrong decision. Find one or two people who genuinely love you, and who have faith-based values, to share your problems with.

I've also shared my problems and weaknesses with one particular friend who gave me wrong advice. If not for God's grace my marriage could have ended. With the benefit of hindsight it really wasn't her fault because she didn't know better at the time. She was speaking from her own perspective and experiences. In her opinion, she may have been doing it out of love, so she can't be blamed. I should have known better.

It is important to know the roles your friends play so you don't make someone who is only meant to be a friend for fun purposes, your confidant.

A **sponsor** is someone who believes in your dream and would go to great lengths to support your dream, even financially. I have many sponsors, including my husband, who invest their time and money in me.

A **Judas** is someone who you know doesn't have your best interest at heart but they pretend to. Some will call them 'haters' or 'frenemies.' Thankfully, God has blessed me with a spirit of discernment so I know the people who are not for me but pretend to be for me. I play along with them without letting them know that I am onto them. I'm careful around them.

It is good to have these people around because they keep me accountable. They remind me that I can't trust just anybody. God will use every Judas in your life for His glory. Judas was pivotal to helping Jesus fulfil His destiny on earth. Jesus didn't send Him away. The key thing, though, is that He was aware.

Even though Joseph's brothers tried to kill him and sold him to slavery, they were used to send him on the path of destiny.

Every relationship in your life has a purpose. That being said, it is important to point out that there are some people you would have to love from afar. Pray to God to show you who these people are.

A **prayer partner** is someone who you meet up with frequently, preferably weekly, to pray together. Whatever you discuss during these sessions should be kept strictly confidential. The times of prayer between my prayer partner and I are some of my most precious and treasured moments. It's been a time of prayer, celebration, tears, and joy.

A **mentee** or mentees are people you guide and teach to walk the path you have walked, or the path you are walking. This is important. The bible puts it this way,

> *"These older women must train the younger women to love their husbands and their children, to live wisely and be pure, to work in their homes, to do good, and to be submissive to their husbands. Then they will not bring shame on the word of God."*
> **Titus 2:4-5 NLT**

We must pass on knowledge and share the lessons of our experiences with the younger generation. Jesus spent time with His disciples. I have been blessed with some of the most amazing mentees. I tend to learn more from them than I even teach.

Make time in your schedule to nurture all your relationships. Some of my friends and I have a Whatsapp group where we chat every day. It's a good way to keep in touch. In my schedule this year, I have included a day every month where I spend a few hours with my friends.

If you don't have any friends, take out time to pray to God to send a friend your way. Also look out for someone who you can be a friend to. I attended the wake keeping of a young woman who died recently. A lady mentioned that she had received an encouraging note from her in church one day, paraphrased, *"Everything will be okay, call me if you need someone to talk to."* They spoke, and the young woman called her everyday to check up on her.

Sometimes, we need to reach out to someone and not wait for someone to reach out to us.

Genette Howard says every woman should have a BFF: Beautiful Faithful Friend.

I agree.

## *Summary*

**The Richer Woman is not alone. She maintains and nurtures important relationships in her life. She reaches out to others and shows them love.**

## *Action Points*

a. Score your friendships/relationships on a scale of 1-10.
b. Why did you rate yourself this score?
c. List five things you are going to do differently to ensure you maintain good relationships. Include dates you would like to achieve these five things.
d. List five things you intend to stop doing to ensure you maintain good relationships. Include dates you intend to stop doing these five things.

# Fun/Recreation/Rest

*"Let her sleep for when she awakes she would move mountains.""*
**Anonymous**

Fun, recreation and rest are very important. Even God rested on the seventh day after working for six days. Jesus also often took time away to just be by Himself.

As women, there is a tendency to overwork ourselves and this is very dangerous. This is more evident in people who are passionate about their work; work is life to them. While it is good to be passionate about work, it is important to draw the line and know when to take a break from work and rest. I once met a lady who had a nervous breakdown and her life changed drastically.

Every woman should have a Sabbath. Monday is my Sabbath. I try not to do anything work-related on Mondays; I also don't take on any client engagements. The only activity I engage in is to pick my kids up from school in the afternoon, and I pray with my prayer partner on Monday afternoons. I don't even shower. It is a day for me to rest and refresh myself with God.

You must find time once a week for yourself. I heard of a woman in America who works, doesn't have help and has kids. Her Sabbath is on Fridays. You must be strict with your Sabbath. I have had to turn down very lucrative work offers because I know that it is important to rest and, once I compromise even once, it would become a habit.

When I used to work in investment banking, my Sabbath was just leaving the house and going to the salon to get my hair done, or a pedicure on Saturdays. Periodic spa treatments and massages are also good.

You must let your husband know that you need this time out. He can take on your responsibilities or watch the kids in that period.

Like I mentioned earlier, my friend and I went away on holiday in 2013. If you can, this is also a great way to rest. It was important for us to spend time alone – after breakfast we went our separate ways so that each person could have time alone – and then we met up again for dinner. You don't have to go far, you can go to a Hotel down the road for a night or two, just to have that time alone.

A woman should also have a good support network in order to be able to rest. When my girls were a lot younger, I would send them to my best friend's house, my mum's or my cousin's house for the weekend. This gave my husband and I time alone to rest.

Please, it is important to be careful where you send your kids. There are so many predators around. My best friend doesn't have any male staff in her home and neither do I, so I am comfortable sending my girls to hers. I also have regular sexual awareness talks with my girls, so I would always warn them never to interact with male staff. Our laundry man of about 20 years doesn't come into the house, and neither do my drivers. When you have daughters you must be extra careful.

Time out with your girlfriends is also needed. Vacations are important. My ideal situation would be to go on different vacations annually: one on my own, one with my husband, one with my husband and kids and one with my girlfriends. This is one of my goals.

Lastly, it is important to sleep early and wake up early. The Bible says :

> *It is vain for you to rise up early, to sit up late, to eat the bread of sorrows; for so He gives His beloved sleep."*
> **Psalm 127:2 NKJV**

Remember whose you are and how precious you are to Him, and rest.

## *Summary*

**The Richer Woman is someone who knows the importance of fun and rest. She makes time to let her hair down, have fun and replenish.**

## *Action Points*

a. Score your current rest habits on a scale of 1-10.
b. Why did you rate yourself this score?
c. List five things you are going to do differently to ensure you make out time to have fun and rest. Include dates you would like to achieve these five things.
d. List five things you intend to stop doing to ensure you have fun and rest properly. Include dates you would like to stop doing these five things.

# Money/Finances

*"She considers a field and buys it: From her profit she plants a vineyard."*.
**Proverbs 31 NIV**

When you saw the title of this book, you thought it was a book about money, right? Well, just like in this book, money is only a small element in the grand scheme of things. It is just one aspect of wealth.

Money was such an idol for me. All I ever wanted was to have plenty of it. I thought it would solve my problems. In this walk of purpose, God has taught me a lot about money. God has a sense of humour. For someone who made money an idol and then decided not to pursue it any longer, God then asks me to talk about it and makes me an authority.

There's a lot of information available on how to make, manage and grow your money. These are very important. "The Richer Woman" should have control of her finances just as the Proverbs 31 woman did. I have a blog dedicated to this (*www.pocketfinance101.blogspot.com*); however, for the purpose of this book, I will focus on two aspects of money that are rarely talked about. Many financial experts usually ignore this and so I will dwell on it in this book.

These two aspects are: the mind-set (what money is) and how to use money.

## So, What Is Money?

I've learnt that money is inconsequential in the grand scheme of things. God doesn't need money to do His work. Did He use money to create the earth? No, He didn't. Money was created by man, and the idea and wisdom for it came from God. However, people have replaced their love for God with the love and pursuit of money.

Does this mean money is evil? By all means, no. It is just a tool, a tool to be used for God's purposes.

It is the love for money that is evil; this is what we call mammon. This is the reason for the downfall of so many. Many people are serving mammon and they don't even realise it.

Almost every major decision taken by individuals or family is based on money. People do not walk in purpose because of money. People seek money by all means. Many people fail to fulfil God's dreams or plans for them because of money. Families are breaking down because of money.

Let me give you a few scenarios.

The reason why many children are neglected by their parents is because of the pursuit of money. They need to survive and so they choose careers that will fund their expenses, at the expense of having time to bring up their children. Many people, like myself, chose certain careers because of the pursuit of money and not because they were called to be in that career. I chose a career in investment banking when I should have chosen a career in media, motivational speaking and life coaching.

I know many people who could make a huge difference in the agricultural sector in Nigeria, but they are stuck in jobs in banking and oil and gas, because it is quicker and easier to make money in these careers. They are depriving the world of their God-given talents.

I know a lady who worked in an oil and gas company, but today she is a creative food entrepreneur. She has come up with the most creative foods. I know another lady who was a lawyer and the general manager of a school, and today, she is a world-renowned weight loss coach. She has impacted so many people with her gift. I know another lawyer who is now a chef with a specialty in pastry. Her desserts are the best in Nigeria, as far as I'm concerned.

One thing they all have in common is that they are walking in purpose. They would have deprived the world of their God-given gifts if they didn't fulfil purpose. The amazing thing is that they are very successful in their businesses and are making very good money, way more than they earned in their previous careers. The beauty about it is that they are fulfilled.

When you chase money, it will never come to you. It will never be enough.

But when you walk in purpose, the entire universe will conspire to work in your favour. Money will chase you. It is like a current, it flows to where value is being created. Do the birds have money? Yet they eat every day. Do the lions have money? Yet they never go hungry.

God has given many people dreams or visions, but they don't make it a reality because they are looking at the money – or lack of it – in their bank accounts. But wherever there is vision, provision will follow. Vision precedes provision.

It's like the analogy of a seed:

A seed is made up of three parts. The largest part is called the endosperm, which is where food is stored. When the seed is planted in the soil, it first of all feeds on its internal food storage in the endosperm, then, as it grows, it begins to attract the nutrients in the soil, and then water. As it grows and begins to grow out of the soil, it begins to attract sunlight.

This is how we should finance our dreams: First of all, what is your value proposition? What value can you create? Then you can start small with whatever you have. Most successful entrepreneurs started with nothing, and they say that the lack of money enabled them to be innovative.

Let me give you two examples. A friend of mine was inspired to start the first of its kind air ambulance service in Nigeria and West Africa after the death of her sister. To run an air ambulance service, you need a private jet or a helicopter. She didn't have the funds for this and she came up with an innovative idea. She realized that many rich Nigerians had private jets and many of these jets were not being used often. It actually costs more money to keep your jet on ground than in the air. She decided to approach them to include their jets in a pool, and whenever she required a jet for an emergency she would reach out to her pool of private jet owners and lease whichever one was available. It was a win-win situation because these jet owners could earn money even when they weren't using their jets. And for my friend, she got paid for it, and used the proceeds to pay to lease the planes. If she had allowed the lack of money to stop her from fulfilling her dreams, many lives would not have been saved today.

We were meant to work on a project together and she was reluctant for us to start with too much capital. She said the principles she'd learnt when her business was still in its infancy are the same principles she imbibes today, and this is one of the reasons for her continued success.

The second example is when I started selling Arabian tunics. I didn't have to start with any money of my own, the supplier gave me the products for sale and when I sold them I would pay her the cost and keep the profit for myself.

I have also hosted three conferences at expensive venues. My last conference was hosted at the most expensive venue in my country. I didn't have the money to pay for this; in fact, I had nothing. I was terrified when I felt God say I should use that venue. How was I going to pay for it? The only reason I had the audacity to even go to the venue to inquire about the cost and to eventually book it is because God and I have history and I know that when He gives a vision, He will make provision; my own responsibility is just to obey.

Then the most amazing thing happened.

See, about three years ago, I was invited to speak to a small group of ladies. A small group of friends had started a monthly meet-up where they would also invite a speaker to come and share with them on a topic, and they invited me to speak. It was not very convenient for me, especially since I wasn't getting paid. It was early days in my career but I knew I needed to go and sow a seed. I had no idea how that seed would bear fruit. I found out that the lady in charge of banqueting at the venue was one of the ladies I coached in the house that day; in fact it was her house I had gone to speak!

When I walked into the administrative office, I immediately got a 50% discount. I was allowed to bring in my own food and drinks, which is never done because that is where the organisation makes their money. On the day of the event, when I walked into the venue, they had added another complimentary hall to the hall I'd paid for!

That's not even the end of my testimony. God made a way and I paid for the venue in full a few days before the event, and I was overwhelmed with His love when I walked into the hall. Then, toward the end of the event God asked me to share the testimony of the venue. I did, and the next day a lady sent me a direct message on Instagram saying that the Holy Spirit had told her to give me all the money she made after she lost her job two weeks ago. I checked my account and it was beyond my wildest imagination. I was at the bank when I read the message and when I checked my account and saw what she had deposited, I screamed and ran out of the bank in awe. I was with one of my mentees and she cried when I shared the news with her. I am still in awe.

What is that thing God is asking you to do? Is the lack of money still stopping you?

One of the things I've learnt about money is that the amount of money you have in your bank account doesn't earn you respect. God began to open doors for me to talk about money at some of the biggest platforms at a time when I had little or none of it. A year after I left investment banking, I was invited to speak at one of the world's biggest consulting firms with other organisations with billions of dollars' worth of assets under their management, one of which was the company I had worked in. I honestly felt like a big fraud. Like, "Really, God?" I was speaking about money to people who had tons more money than me.

God has completely demystified the myth called money. There is currently a recession going on in Nigeria as I write this book but I am not afraid. In fact, I don't want the recession to end for selfish reasons. It is working in my favour and is one of the best times for me in my business and ministry. There are so many opportunities, even in this recession.

Last year, I spent some time with God while I did the Daniel fast and I asked Him a few questions. I was concerned with the number of people losing their jobs because of the recession. I asked Him to show me where He was at work so I could join Him. God began to tell me that these people would end up being entrepreneurs. This recession was going to work in our favour.

God began to show me the opportunities in a neglected sector in Nigeria, agriculture. Nigeria is a blessed country; we have arable land, 80% of which is not in use. We have abundant water resources. We have a large youthful population and very good weather conditions. Everything grows in Nigeria. Despite these great attributes, we import almost everything in Nigeria. We spend over $500 million annually, importing tomato paste, when tomato is grown in Nigeria – but with a 60% post-harvest loss. It just doesn't make sense. The sad thing is that many of the people who can revive the sector are stuck in jobs in the banking sector and oil and gas companies because of the instant or quick rewards they could get. Some of them are out of work, but they won't go into agriculture because it is not seen as a job of preference.

God asked me to host an agribusiness entrepreneurship workshop where we showcased the opportunities in the sector. Today, many agribusinesses have sprung up as a result of this workshop. These entrepreneurs are thriving even in the recession. One of the entrepreneurs watched the recording of the workshop and was inspired to start a packaging company. Today, he has helped produce world-class packaging for Nigerian brands. He has so much work that he has had to turn down work. We are creating wealth for Nigeria and Africa and we will help alleviate the risk of global food security.

The Bible doesn't lie when it says in *"But remember the Lord for it is He who gives you the power to get wealth"* (**Deuteronomy 8:18**).

Many people pursue money when they should really be seeking God. He is the creator of the universe and all that is in it. All the gold, diamond, rubies, pearls and other precious elements were created by Him. He created the richest man who ever lived, King Solomon.

King Solomon reigned for 40 years. Each year he received 25 tons of gold. Some estimates say 1 ton is worth $64.3million, and 25 tones multiplied by 40 years is $64 billion. This does not even include the following:

- His inheritance from his father, King David.
- Gold and silver received from the kings of Arabia, governors and merchants.
- The heavy taxes paid by the Israelites.
- Tribute money from countries and kingdoms.
- Gold, silver, ivory, apes, monkeys, Ethiopians, and peacocks received every three years due to his business partnership with Hiram, King of Tyre.
- The gifts of gold, spices, precious stones, garments, armour, horses, mules, and so on, that he received each year.

I read somewhere else that, taking his father, King David's wealth into consideration and his own wealth, Kong Solomon was worth $222 trillion.

The second richest man in the history of the world is John Rockefeller. His net worth is calculated at $400 billion. He was a devoted Christian.

The world's richest man is Bill Gates with a net worth of $75 billion as at March 2016 by Forbes and $85 billion dollars as at July 2016 by Bloomberg. This is nothing compared to John Rockefeller's wealth, not to talk of comparing it to King Solomon's wealth.

George Washington Carver is known as the man of science and a man of God. He discovered 100 uses for sweet potatoes and 300 uses for peanuts.

Some of the greatest brands were created by Christians. For example, Quaker Oats, Heinz, Coca-Cola, Mary Kay and Tropicana. These brands have outlived their founders. In recent times, successful brands such as HTC, Forever 21, In and Out burger, and Chick Fil A were founded by Christians. Many of these founders attribute their success to God.

Truly, it is God who gives the power to get wealth. If many people realized this truth, they would stop chasing money and begin to chase God.

> *Therefore I say to you, do not worry about your life, what you will eat or what you will drink; nor about your body, what you will put on. Is not life more than food and the body more than clothing? Look at the birds of the air, for they neither sow nor reap nor gather into barns; yet your heavenly Father feeds them. Are you not of more value than they? Which of you by worrying can add one cubit to his stature? "So why do you worry about clothing? Consider the lilies of the field, how they grow: they neither toil nor spin; and yet I say to you that even Solomon in all his glory was not arrayed like one of these. Now if God so clothes the grass of the field, which today is, and tomorrow is thrown into the oven, will He not much more clothe you, O you of little faith? "Therefore do not worry, saying, 'What shall we eat?' or 'What shall we drink?' or 'What shall we wear?' For after all these things the Gentiles seek. For your heavenly Father knows that you need all these things. But seek first the kingdom of God and His righteousness, and all these things shall be added to you. Therefore do not worry about tomorrow, for tomorrow will worry about its own things. Sufficient for the day is its own trouble.*
> **Matthew 6:25-34 NKJV**

At the end of the day, it is important to know that, truly, when you make all this money, you won't take it with you when you die. It is better to store up treasures in Heaven.

> *Do not lay up for yourselves treasures on earth, where moth and rust destroy and where thieves break in and steal; but lay up for yourselves treasures in heaven, where neither moth nor rust destroys and where thieves do not break in and steal. For where your treasure is, there your heart will be also."*
>
> Matthew 6:19 – 21 ESV

## How To Use Money

Money can be used for good. There is a quote that *says, "Where the purpose of a thing is not known, abuse is inevitable."* It's all about knowing the purpose of money.

When you make all this money, is it to buy nice things, live in the best houses and go on expensive holidays? While there is nothing wrong with these things, this is not the purpose of money. Money is to be used as a tool in God's kingdom.

Let me give you an example. The current mortality rate of breast cancer in Nigeria is high. According to statistics, over 90% of the people who are diagnosed with breast cancer die. In countries like the US and the UK, the reverse is the case, because they are able to detect the disease early.

We do not have enough diagnostic centres In Nigeria.

I remember when we needed to do a brain scan for my mum, I contacted one of my doctor friends and we were told that there were only two MRI scan machines working in a state that has a population of over 20 million people. When we got to one of the hospitals, we were told that the MRI scan wasn't working and so she had to have a CT scan. What is even more alarming is that these are private hospitals and, for my mum to even be attended to, we were asked to deposit a ridiculously huge sum of money and at 8pm at night. What happens to the millions of citizens at the lower end of the pyramid who can't even afford to eat on a daily basis?

Now, this where a Christian can use the wealth that they have been blessed with to buy many scan machines that would save millions of people.

Many people have been displaced because of the insurgency in Northern Nigeria, and because of the wars in Syria and other countries. They need food, water, clothing, shelter and healthcare. This is where we can use the wealth we have been blessed with.

Many orphans are dying of AIDS. There are far too many problems in the world.

If a believer uses his or her wealth to help one of these causes, or to solve one of these problems, this person has the potential to win many souls. They can use the opportunity to witness about the love of Jesus to the people that they help. You cannot preach to me about Jesus when you can't even meet my immediate needs.

When you make money–or if you already have money– ask God what He intends for you to do with it. We are just conduits that money should flow through. Where the purpose of a thing is not known, abuse is inevitable. Where the purpose of money is not known, abuse is inevitable.

As I close this section, it's important to state that we must give to God and honour Him with our first fruit. We must give Him what belongs to Him. We must give Him at least a tenth of our earnings; this is called a Tithe.

I give more than ten percent, and I have heard of people who give God ninety percent of their earnings. You may think that it is crazy, but it is not.

God owes no man.

As an entrepreneur, I pay tithe on my profit and sometimes I also pay on revenues. When I was a salary earner, I also used to pay tithe on my gross earnings and not my net earnings. I remember asking someone's opinion on this and the person said, "Which would you prefer, blessings on gross earnings or blessings on net?" That sealed it for me.

I also give the first fruit of my earnings. When I launch a new business or product, I give God the first proceeds. For example, when I officially started my coaching business, I gave God one hundred percent of the first payment from my first client for the first month.

In all of this, it is important to be led by the Holy Spirit.

Just like the Proverbs 31 woman, it is important to imbibe good financial principles. It is important to save, budget, invest, pay off debt, and give.

## Summary

**The Richer Woman is a woman who is in charge of her finances. She knows the purpose of money and uses it wisely.**

## Action Points

a. Score yourself on a scale of 1-10 with regards to your finances.
b. Why did you rate yourself this score?
c. List five things you are going to do differently to ensure you improve on your finances and have a healthy relationship with money. Include a date when you intend to achieve these five things.

d. List five things you will stop doing to ensure you improve on your finances and have a healthy relationship with money. Include a date when you intend to stop doing these five things.

# Time Management

*"Time is the most valuable coin in your life. You and you alone will determine how that coin will be spent. Be careful that you do not let other people spend it for you."*
**Carl Sandburg**

Time management is an important attribute "The Richer Woman" must possess, especially since we have diverse responsibilities.

God is a God of order. Every single day the sun rises and sets at the exact time God has determined. In order to be able to fully fulfil your role as "The Richer Woman", you must be able to manage your time effectively. It is an area I am working on and intend to keep improving in. I have applied some of the following methods in the past:

I have used a time management tool from the Masterlife discipleship course called Master time. I have also worked with weekly to-do lists, which I break further into daily to-do lists. I find that setting reminders is also helpful. I have also used a yearly planner, and I just bought the book, Eat That Frog, by Brian Tracy. It helps with procrastination and time management.

It is still very difficult to keep to this routine and there are also things that are out of your control, but it is important not to beat yourself up too much over not keeping strictly to your routine. It is really just a guide.

A good way to apportion your time is to list all your roles. Under each role, list out your activities or responsibilities and then apportion how much time you need to accomplish each one. Then, you can schedule the time you intend to achieve this.

For instance, in my role as a mother, one of my activities or responsibilities is to spend time reading the Bible with my kids. I know that this takes approximately thirty minutes each day, so I schedule thirty minutes before they go to bed during the week. We often forget to do this on Friday and Saturday night but I hope to improve on this.

There is such an information overload in these times we live in, especially with technology, so it is important to schedule your time. I've come to realise that I haven't been able to read as many books as I used to, because of time spent on social media. At the beginning of the year, I took the first month off interacting on social media and in that period, I was able to finish reading four books. I was also able to finish the first draft of this book.

At the same time, everything must be done in moderation. We must be flexible enough to allow the Holy Spirit lead and disrupt our time schedule.

It is also important to give God the first fruit of your time, whether daily, monthly or weekly. I try to wake up before everyone else to have quiet time with God. As I mentioned earlier, I also take out Monday as my Sabbath to rest and spend time with God. I also take time out in January to just spend time with God in the first month of the year.

When you give God the first fruit of your time, He will bless the rest of your times.

It is important to set your priorities and to focus, and it.

It is also important for me to point that you shouldn't be too hard on yourself because you will fall and make mistakes in the process. The most important thing is to get back up when you fall.

## *Summary*

**The Richer Woman knows that time is one of her most valuable assets. She knows she will have to account for the time she has been given on earth. She knows that in order to fulfil purpose, she must be a good steward of her time. She manages her time effectively and lives a productive life.**

## *Action Points*

a. Score yourself on a scale of 1-10 with regard to managing your time and being organised.
b. Why did you rate yourself this score?
c. List five things you are going to do differently to ensure you are organised and use your time wisely. Include a date you would like to achieve these five things.
d. List five things you will stop doing to ensure you are better organized and use your time wisely. Include a date you intend to stop doing these things.

# Why People Don't Become the Richer Woman

Many women are aware of the beauty and benefits of being "The Richer Woman." Many women would like to live purposeful lives; they would like to resign from careers that do not allow them to be all that God has created them to be. They'd like to be great wives and mothers, and they would like to live the Richer life.

But the sad thing is that many women do not become "The Richer Woman." Like the statistics of the moth and butterfly, there are still many more women living like moths.

But if the advantages of living the Richer life are so obvious, why don't people choose that path?

One major reason for this is fear, and fear manifests in different forms.

## What is Fear?

You may have heard that FEAR is an acronym for: False Evidence Appearing Real. Unfortunately, this is the reality for many women. I listened to a podcast by one of my mentors, Terri Savelle Foy, and she told a hilarious story showing just how easy it is for us to believe false evidence that appears real.

Every morning around 5am, she goes jogging on a path she really likes.

One morning, a group of women stopped her abruptly. They told her not to go down her usual route because there was a skunk there that could attack her. She thought to herself, "There's no way I'm going to get attacked by a skunk!" and decided to change her jogging path. After a few days, she really missed her original path because the new route was narrow and not as nice. She thought to herself, "What if those ladies were lying?"

That morning, she proceeded on her original path. As she was jogging, she saw a black object with white stripes and she freaked out. She ran for her life, even dropping her phone in the process and praying silently. Then, later that morning, she was driving out with her daughter and saw the same object in the same position. She wondered why the skunk hadn't moved an inch and decided to take a closer look. Upon getting there, she realized it was a baseball and not a skunk.

Surely the FEAR of the skunk had prevented her from following the path she loved dearly.

Fear is an emotion and, as with every emotion, it has its good and bad sides.

Fear can be a good thing; its purpose is to prevent us from harming ourselves or to keep us from danger. For instance, fear would stop you from crossing the road abruptly or going near an animal like a lion. Now, the problem arises when you let fear paralyse you and prevent you from fulfilling God's purpose for your life, and pursuing your dreams.

As humans, we are born with only two types of fear: Fear of falling and fear of loud noises.[21] My son is 22 months old as at the time I am writing this book and, when he was

---

[21] Kounang, Nadia. "What is the science behind fear?" CNN. Retrieved February 14, 2017, from http://edition.cnn.com/2015/10/29/health/science-of-fear/

much younger, he would fret and spread out his arms whenever we threw him up. This is because he was afraid of falling. Also, if a baby hears a loud noise, it would fret. But, aside from these, a baby is generally not fearful. A baby will put his or her hand into fire, jump off a building or play with a knife.

All other fears are fears we have learned or that have been programmed into us through negative beliefs or culture.

> *For God has not given us a spirit of fear, but of power, and of love and of a sound mind.*
> **2 Timothy 1:7 NKJV**

God is love. He is perfect love.

If God is love and love dwells in us, that means God dwells in us and there is no place for fear. God and fear cannot dwell in the same place.

Types of fear people face:

## Fear Of Failure:

> *"And you ask, 'What if I fall?'*
> *Oh, but my darling,*
> *What if you fly?"*
> **Erin Hanson**

When it was time for me to leave investment banking, I was petrified. I was so afraid of leaving my comfort zone. I was afraid of stepping out into the unknown. The fact that I was resigning from investment banking after many years of working in finance made me feel like a failure. I thought I had wasted all that time. Now I was stepping into the unknown. What if I failed?

When God asked me to write this book, to talk about my personal life – some of the things I have been through and the mistakes I have made – I was so afraid; what would people say, what would they think?

But it is okay to fail; failure is a necessary part of the process to success. We are created to learn by failure.

How does a baby learn how to walk? The child tries to stand up, falls down, tries again, takes a few steps, falls down again and, before you know it, the child is running around. The only way you learn how to do anything is to fail at it. Then, from the previous experiences, you'll know how not to do it, next time. As Peter Drucker says, "Fail fast, fail first and fail often."

Most of the world's most successful people were experts at failing. Walt Disney was fired by a newspaper editor because he "lacked imagination and had no good ideas." This is just one of the many setbacks he faced in life. When he tried to get MGM studios to distribute Mickey Mouse in 1927, he was told that the idea wouldn't work, because "a giant mouse on a screen would terrify women."[22]

Bill Gates and Steve Jobs dropped out of school. Thomas Edison made at least a thousand attempts to create the light bulb.

At a conference I attended in 2014, my aunt shared the story of how she failed to attract investors for her hotel project and, after about 7 years of trying, she gave up. Shortly

---

[22] Weisman, Aly. "14 people who failed before becoming super successful stars." Business Insider. Retrieved February 24, 2017, from http://business.financialpost.com/business-insider/14-people-who-failed-before-becoming-super-successful-stars

after, her dream investor came on board. Today, her hotel has been number one on the Trip Advisor list for Lagos.

Famous failures include: Steve Jobs, Michael Jordan, Oprah Winfrey, Bill Gates, Mark Zuckerberg, Strive Masiyiwa, Hilary Clinton and Omilola Oshikoya.

Failure should be perceived as a teacher. The very fact that you are failing at something is evidence that you are trying something new.

**Also, it is important to note that, when you are walking in Gods will for you and when you are being obedient to God's instructions, failure is not an option. You cannot fail with God.**

# Fear Of Trading Security For The Unknown

After I informed my ex CEO that I was leaving the company I'd loved so much, he was intrigued. He wanted to speak with me because, when someone wants to take a leap of faith like I was, certainly that person must be on to something, and he proceeded to tell me his own story.

When he was about 31, he resigned from a well-paid job. He wanted to come back to Nigeria to do something in the asset management space. This was about 20 years ago when the financial industry in Nigeria was very premature. He was leaving the security of a stable, well-paid job, for the unknown. Today, this company is the largest non-bank financial institution in Nigeria.

I love this quote by John A Shedd that says, *"A ship in harbour is safe, but that is not what ships are built for."* Ships are built for the high seas. It is when they are on water that they fulfil their purpose. Sometimes, in this place of purpose, a ship would have to go through storms. Yes, some may not make it past the storms, but most of them make it through.

They get to experience the beauty of the world and reach destinations that they would not have, if they had stayed in the harbour.

Is there really anything that is 'known'? Due to the recent recession in Nigeria, and the financial crisis in the world, many who thought they had secure jobs in some of the best companies in the world have lost their jobs. Many of these companies have failed and been shut down.

Really, nothing is secure.

## Fear of what others would say or think.

A lot of people live their lives to fulfil other people's dreams. An example of this is studying medicine because your father is a doctor, or getting married to a particular person because of parental pressure. People who do this are the ones who typically fit into this category of fear; their fear of what their loved ones would think is what limits them.

I read an article about a hospice worker who shared on the Top 5 regrets of the dying. The most common regret was, "I wish I'd had the courage to live a life true to myself, not the life others expected of me."[23]

Life is precious. You only have one life to live. There is no dress rehearsal; this is the real thing. Why don't you live the life you want to live, so that you don't end up like those referenced by the hospice worker?

For me, it is a matter of heaven or hell. When I first started writing this book, I started writing a generic book but God began to reveal that it was a book for women. When I

---

[23] Steiner, Susan. "Top five regrets of the dying." The Guardian. Retrieved February 24, 2017, from https://www.theguardian.com/lifeandstyle/2012/feb/01/top-five-regrets-of-the-dying

realised He wanted me to share things like cheating on my husband, I was scared. I knew that there would come a time when I had to share the story of how God gave me beauty from ashes, but I didn't think it would be now. Lord, how can I share this? Many women like Joyce Meyer had shared stories of abuse or divorce, but no one had ever shared a story on adultery. What would people say? What would people think?

One day I was sleeping and I saw **1st John Chapter 2 verse 4** on a sheet of paper. I woke up saying the scripture and was excited to check it out; surely, God had a word of encouragement for me. But I was shocked to *read, "He who says, 'I know Him" and does not keep His commandments, is a liar, and the truth is not in Him."*

Ouch. The truth hurts, but it is so accurate. How can I say I love Him but fail to keep His commandments? In the time since then, God has been talking to me about obedience: it is a matter of Heaven and hell. God showed me something profound in **Matthew Chapter 25 verses 14-30**, something I had never noticed even though I had read this story many times; it is about a master who gave his servant talents.

The Master gave one person five talents, gave another one two and gave the last person one talent. The first two servants were faithful with the talents he gave them, but the last servant with only one talent buried it.

His reason for burying it? He was afraid.

All the times I had read this parable, I'd stopped where the master took the one talent away from the servant and gave it to the one who had five talents and had multiplied it into ten. What I never noticed was that in verse 30, it says, *"And cast the unprofitable servant into the outer darkness. There will be weeping and gnashing of teeth."* I did some research and found out that 'outer darkness' means hell.

Our lack of obedience to our call to fulfil purpose, to use the gifts and talents that God has given us, can lead us to hell.

I was invited to speak at Google and when I was signing autographs for my journal, a lady came up to me and said, "There is a book you are writing. God says you should speed it up. This book will save many marriages."

I may be afraid of the people who will persecute me as I have opened up and shared my mistakes, but I know that millions of lives will be changed, many marriages will be restored and many will seek a deeper relationship with Jesus.

Who cares about what those people say, anyway? Do they determine if I wake up every morning? Do they determine where I will spend eternity? Are they perfect? Have they never made mistakes?

> *"I trust in God, so why should I be afraid? What can mere mortals do to me?"*
> **Psalm 56:11 NLT**

> *"And do not fear those who kill the body but cannot kill the soul. But rather fear Him who is able to destroy both soul and body in hell."*
> **Matthew 10:28 ESV**

## Fear Of Not Being Able To Cope Financially

I believe this may be the most common fear. Trust me, you'll be fine. You will just have to make some adjustments – it's all about delayed gratification, as opposed to instant satisfaction. Would you rather pay now and play later or play now and pay later?

This was one of my greatest fears. I mentioned earlier that, when I was ready to leave investment banking, I earned more than my husband and I was afraid we wouldn't be able to cope financially. I was also afraid that my childhood fears would come to pass, since my husband works in a family law firm, just like my father had worked for his father's company. Let me just say that God has done exceedingly and abundantly above all I could ever imagine or think.

Initially, it was tough, but God worked on my character and taught me many profound things during that period. He taught me to depend on Him daily for everything. This is why, even in a recession, I'm not afraid because I have known Jehovah Jireh, God our provider.

He also taught me to be humble: I had to rely on my husband and it taught me humility. I began to respect him more. Prior to this, if something happened to my car, for example, I would be quick to fix it on my own, but now I needed my husband. He now felt needed by me and joyously did so much for me. His wife now needed him! I allowed him to perform his God-given role, which was to provide for me and take care of me.

We also learnt to appreciate the simple things in life. We learnt to enjoy our own company without distractions. For Valentine's Day, instead of going to fancy restaurants, I would cook dinner for my husband and the kids. My husband said once, during our discipleship class, that we might not have as much cash as we had when I was in investment banking, but now he had more peace of mind.

What little we had now lasted even more. God multiplied what we had and we had so much food to eat. I was worried about health insurance, but did I want good health or good healthcare?

There were many tests - once, my mum suffered a stroke and we were required to pay a huge sum of money as a deposit at the hospital. I felt really sad that I couldn't pay for it, I felt that I would have been able to afford it if I hadn't left my job. But God is so awesome; He made a way where there was no way.

Through the process, God also opened mind-blowing doors for my husband. All the things we have wanted to do, we have been able to do.

God has also opened doors for me; my business is doing very well. Yes, there may be tough times, but tough times don't last; they only help you develop the muscles of greatness.

My perspective has changed on a lot of things. I no longer care for things that don't have eternal value. And yet, God has blessed me with the most amazing things without me having to pay a dime. I have received some of the most expensive designer shoes as gifts! Truly, when you seek Him first, all other things will be added. I remember once thinking it was time to get a new handbag. I began to think of which bag to get but then a friend of mine called and told me that God said she should give me a bag, and it was a Christian Dior bag.

Some may think this is charity. Trust me, it is not charity; these things are inconsequential in the grand scheme of things. As I walk in purpose, God sends whatever I need just like He did for Jesus while He was on earth.

Let me use an analogy: when you go shopping you usually receive a gift or a free item. For instance, you buy one item and get the other free. Do you go shopping asking to buy the free item? No, you just focus on the original purchase and take what comes with it. Many people are focusing on the extras when they should be focusing on purpose.

Let us change the definition of fear from False Evidence Appearing Real to Future Expectations Appearing Real.

I love the lyrics to the song Oceans (Where feet may fail) by Hillsong. It talks about God calling us out into deep waters, where we can no longer rely on our feet, and have to rely on faith in God.

Becoming The Richer Woman is like going out into the deep. It often feels like walking on water.

**What do you do when the fear won't go away?**

**You face your fears and DO IT AFRAID.**

## Action Points

a. Are you going to let fear stop you from fulfilling purpose?
b. Which one of the fears listed above is holding you back?
c. What is the worst thing that can happen if you decide to take a step of faith?
d. Ask yourself, what would you do if you knew you wouldn't fall or fail?
e. Decide to do it.
f. Set a date to start doing it.

# Be The Richer Woman: Do It Afraid

*"Do it afraid. Jump and build your
wings on the way down."*
**Paul Martinelli.**

The eagle is a very fascinating bird, one of the most intelligent creatures created by God. There are so many wonderful attributes of the eagle but, for the purpose of this book, I will focus on one.

The eagle has only one mating partner for its entire lifetime. Before it chooses its life partner, it goes through a very interesting process of courtship.

The female eagle flies up in the air and drops a stick, which the male eagle would have to catch.

The female eagle does this several times, and at different heights. Sometimes it drops the stick from really great heights, and sometimes it drops the stick from lower heights. If the male eagle is able to catch it consistently, the female chooses it as its spouse.

Now, when the eagle has her eaglets, she makes the nest very comfortable. She cushions the nest with hay and includes sticks and stones for the eaglets to play with. Then when the eaglet is ready to learn to fly, she removes all the nice things and replaces them with thorns, so that the eaglet is no longer comfortable in its nest, then she carries her child to a height and drops it.

The poor eaglet tries to flap its wings, but the first couple of trials are futile because it doesn't yet know how to fly - this is where the eagle that she chose as her life partner comes into play.

When the mother eagle drops the eaglet, it is the job of the father eagle to catch it before it hits the ground.

This process goes on several times until the eaglet learns how to fly.

The mother eagle must be petrified about having to drop her eaglet. What if it falls?

But what if it flies.

Even if she is afraid, she chooses to do it afraid, because her child's ability to fly is dependent on her decision to do it afraid.

Like the eagle, we must face our fears and become the Richer Woman.

Here are some of the things you need to do in order to be able to do it afraid and be the richer woman.

## 1. Have Vision

> *"Vision is the art of seeing what is invisible to others."*
> **Jonathan Swift**

You must have a clear and compelling vision, and you must keep your eyes on the goal.

One animal we can learn this from is the lion:

Humans can only see silhouettes when it's dark, but the lion can see colours even in the dark. The white patches of fur under the eyes of the lion act like reflectors and allow light to come into the eye. This means that the lion is able to see and to maintain its focus, night and day.

We must be like the lion. No matter what is going on around us, we must have a clear vision.

> *"Write the vision and make it plain on tablets, that he may run who reads it. For the vision is yet for an appointed time; But at the end it will speak, and it will not lie. Though it tarries, wait for it; because it will surely come, it will not tarry."*
> **Habakkuk 2:2-3 NKJV**

Do you have a vision board? It is pretty easy to create one. Just get a piece of cardboard. Cut out pictures of things that represent your vision and stick them on the cardboard. Place the cardboard in an area where you can see your vision often.

There are also numerous apps that allow you to do this. I downloaded Terri Savelle Foy's Dream and Goals app. I also have a vision board.

You can have visions for different aspects of your life, and you can create several vision boards to reflect that. But most importantly, it is important to write down God's vision for you and not your own vision for yourself.

## 2. Change Your Belief System

I recently read an interesting story about the elephant in one of John Maxwell's books. Do you know how trainers control massive, 5-ton elephants, and keep them from running away?

When the elephants are babies, the trainers tie one of the elephant's feet to a wooden post that is secured in the ground. The elephant tries to get away but, because it is not yet strong, it is unable to break away, and it gives up.

From that moment on, whenever the elephant's leg is secured, it believes it cannot get away – even though it is able to, and has been able to for a long time.

We humans are like that. We are programmed by our self-belief. We are limited by our thinking, and what limits us is fear. However, fear is a thief and will limit us from breaking away from those false beliefs; it will limit us from accomplishing our God-given desires.

Imagine this: I hate flying but I love travelling. So, for me to get on a plane, I have to make myself see the benefits of travelling and the wonderful places I would not get to see if I give into my fear of flying. I have to program my mind to focus on the benefits and not the fear.

One way to change your belief system is to believe what God says about you.

> "I can do all things through Christ who
> strengthens me."
> **Philippians 4:13 NKJV**

The most important belief that will change all false beliefs is this: you can do all things through Christ.

Build your faith. Think positive thoughts. Stay away from negative people. You must ensure that you're always in a positive and conducive environment, and surround yourself with people who believe in you.

Also, always celebrate your victories, even the small ones. Remembering God's faithfulness in the little things, builds up our faith for the bigger ones. Remember, He has not given you a Spirit of fear but of power, of love and of a sound mind.

## 3. Believe In Yourself And Believe In Your Dreams

> *"You cannot out-perform your own self-belief."*
> **Paul Martinelli**

The Bible says in **Proverbs Chapter 23 verse 7**, *"For as he thinks in his heart, so is he."*

If you take an orange and cut it into two equal halves, you will notice that there are at least a dozen seeds in each orange. Each seed has a potential to become a tree, bearing fruits that contain seeds of their own. So, assuming an orange has a dozen seeds, this means this orange has the potential to produce a dozen trees with countless numbers of oranges and seeds, in its lifetime.

The same logic can be applied in other fruits.

In **Genesis Chapter 1 verse 11**, God said, *"Let the earth put forth vegetation: plants yielding seed and fruit trees yielding fruit whose seed is in itself, each according to its kinds, upon the earth."*

Now, if God took time out to put so many seeds in a common fruit, how much more would He do for us who are created in His image?

> *"God created man in His own image, in the image and likeness of God He created him; male*

> *and female He created them: and God blessed them, and said to them, be fruitful, multiply and fill the earth and subdue it and have dominion over the fish of the seas, the birds of the air and over every living creature that moves upon the earth.".*
>
> **Genesis 1:27-28 NKJV**

The first command or role given to man is to be fruitful and multiply. If God says we should be fruitful and multiply, it means He has deposited many seeds of greatness in us, just as He has done in the case of an orange.

God created you, He blessed you and said you should be fruitful and multiply: it is a command that must be obeyed.

There are hidden resources in you; you cannot even imagine the potential you have. Just visualize the seeds in a single orange fruit and imagine what your own seeds of potential are.

You are greater than that orange. You are not just greater, you are created in the likeness and image of God. Imagine the hidden potential in you! Imagine the great things you have been equipped to do. The greatest men who have walked the earth weren't born with a cape, special DNA or two heads. The difference is that they were aware of their potential and did something about it. They obeyed the command to be fruitful and multiply. We are all gifted and our gifts represent the seeds of greatness the King has deposited in every one of us.

Imagine the potential you have when you have the DNA of Christ in you. You are the daughter of a King. God has given you all the authority you need. He has given you the Helper of helpers, the Holy Spirit.

## 4. Do It Now

Most people, like myself, want to wait until everything is perfect before we act. But remember, while you are waiting for things to be perfect, someone else is already acting and learning from their mistakes.

I read a story in Terri Savelle Foy's book, *Imagine Big*, of a young, struggling actor. He wanted to write a script about a young, underdog boxer who surprised everyone by winning the title, but he thought he was being unrealistic and no one would buy into the story. So he left it. In 1975, he watched a match where a young and relatively unknown underdog, Chuck Wepner, knocked Mohammed Ali to the ground in the 9$^{th}$ round. The match lasted 15 rounds and, even though Mohammed Ali retained his title, the young boxer almost defeated him. The young, struggling actor was inspired by this match, and began to write the script that night. Within three days he was done. That movie won three Oscars and launched the actor into a multi-million dollar career.

That movie is '*Rocky*', and the actor is Sylvester Stallone.

Susan Jeffers says, "Every time you take a step into the unknown, you experience fear. There is no point in saying, 'When I am no longer afraid, then I will do it'; you'll be waiting a long time. The fear is part of the package."

## 5. Take the first step without knowing what lies ahead

This is what I did, and I could not have imagined that it would lead me where I am today.

A year after I resigned, I was invited by one of the world's top consulting firms to speak to its staff on financial planning. I was invited alongside top investment houses in the country, one of which was the company I resigned from. Everyone was surprised that I was the only person representing myself.

Abraham in the Bible didn't know where he was going but he took the first step of faith and, today, we are talking about him thousands of years later. I didn't have a plan but I was secure in God's plan for me.

There is also a place for planning. After about three years of working in the church office, God said it was time to leave. Even though I had left investment banking three years ago, I was still afraid of leaving the church office. We were in the heat of a recession; it didn't make sense to leave. I was also afraid of stepping out again into the unknown, especially when I remembered some of the challenges I had gone through the first time. I went back to God to say, "Well, Lord, you surely won't ask me to do the same thing again."

This time, He took me to **Joshua Chapter 1**.

God told Joshua to leave the wilderness and go to the promise land by crossing the Jordan. When Moses led them out of Egypt, they had had to move immediately, but this time, they had three days to prepare and pack provisions.

> *"Prepare your provisions, for within three days you are to pass over this Jordan to go in to take possession of the land that the Lord your God is giving you to possess."*
> **Joshua 1:11 ESV**

This encouraged me. God specifically gave me a date to leave. It was about three months after He had given me the instruction and, this time, I would have time to prepare.

I also noted that God had asked Joshua to leave the wilderness at a time when the rivers overflowed, a time when there were floods. God said to me, "There is a harvest in the flood. There is a harvest in this recession."

Sometimes you will be required to jump into the unknown without a plan, and sometimes you will be required to plan ahead. It's important to listen closely to the instruction of the Holy Spirit.

## 6. Build A Dream Team

The people in your life will ultimately perform either of two roles: they will either be anchors or motors. Anchors weigh you down, while motors propel you forward.

Like I mentioned in the friendship and relationship section of the Components of The Richer Woman, you need to surround yourself with a dream team:

You need a mentor (someone who has walked the walk and you can look up to), a coach (someone who encourages you), a confidant (someone you can share deep concerns and thoughts with), a buddy (someone you can have fun with or have a laugh with), a sponsor (someone who believes in you, who will sponsor you or find the funds to support you), a Judas (someone to keep you accountable and remind you that you can't share your dreams with the world), a prayer partner (someone to pray with you) and mentees (people you can teach).

You cannot do it alone. Your Dream Team is a crucial part of your journey to fulfilling purpose.

# 7. Stay Motivated

*"People often say that motivation doesn't last. Well, neither does bathing – that's why we recommend it daily."*

**Zig Ziglar**

Motivation is like faith; it fuels our passion and encourages us to stay on the path, even when we face challenges.

There are different ways to stay motivated. A few are:

i. Review your vision often.
ii. Remove all distractions. You may need to unfollow certain people or accounts on social media.
iii. You will need to surround yourself with people who have the same vision as you. For instance, if you hang around people who live for the moment, without any thought for purpose and eternity, you will be tempted to do the same. You may need to change your friends in order to stay motivated about the assignment God has for you.
iv. Ensuring you communicate daily with God helps you stay motivated. God wants us to win, so He will send you encouragement whenever you need it.

# 8. Stay grateful

> *"Count your blessings and stay grateful, even for the little things."*
> **Omilola Oshikoya**

Gratitude is more important than we often realise, and the lack of it is the number one cause of depression in most people. It is easy to get so caught up in where you want to go, that you forget to be grateful for where you've been, where you are at and what you have.

Keep a gratitude list. I was recently given a five-year gratitude journal as a gift and since I've had it, my goal has been to write down what I'm grateful for, each day. Another method is to write down what you are grateful for everyday, and put it in a jar.

Sometimes, when I go through my old journals, I'm just so grateful for all that God has done. It helps me see how far He has brought me.

> *"Take for yourselves twelve stones from here, out of the midst of the Jordan, from the place where the priest's feet stood firm...."*
> *That this may be a sign among you when your children ask in time to come, saying, 'What do these stones mean to you? Then you shall answer them that the waters of the Jordan were cut off before the ark of the covenant of the Lord; when it crossed over the Jordan, the waters of the Jordan were cut off. And these stones shall be for a memorial to the children of Israel forever."*
> **Joshua 4:3, 6-7 NKJV**

It is important to count your blessings and name them one by one.

## 9. Trust The Process

We do not become adults over night. We start of as babies, then toddlers, children, teens and then adults. This process prepares us for the experiences and challenges we will have to go through as adults. The only man who didn't go through this process was Adam, and maybe that's why he failed. Jesus, on the other hand, went through a process.

Look at the story of Joseph. God had given him a vision of greatness, but he went through the process of being sold as a slave, being falsely accused and going to jail, before he became the governor of Egypt. The process prepared him for the place of assignment.

Everything in life has a process. But, unfortunately, we have become an instant satisfaction generation. We want things done overnight, but God is a God of process.

We can learn a lot about process by looking at the Palm Tree.

> *"The righteous shall flourish like a palm tree..."*
> **Psalm 92:3 NKJV**

There are two very popular types of palm trees: the date palm, which grows in the desert, and the coconut tree, which is usually found on sea fronts. For the purpose of this book, I'll focus on the coconut palm tree.

After I read Psalm 92:3, one day, my attention was brought to a coconut tree in the garden at the front of my house. That tree has been there for as long as I have lived there and even longer, but we have never had to water the tree or do anything to it and yet it flourishes. In contrast, there is grass in the same area of the compound and we constantly need to take care of it. So, why does this Palm Tree flourish? I did some research and found out the most amazing things about the Palm Tree.

Some of its attributes are as follows:

- Its leaves are evergreen, 365 days of the year.
- The older the tree, the more abundant, luscious and sweeter its fruit.
- Dust of the earth does not accumulate on the palm tree.
- Palm trees grow taller than many other trees in the plant kingdom, and no other tree can survive near a Palm tree.
- They thrive in sandy soil and have a high tolerance for salinity (salt).
- It produces the largest seed in the plant kingdom, known as the coconut.

Another wonderful thing is that almost every part of the palm tree can be used by humans in some manner, and has significant economic value:

- The roots are used as dye, mouthwash and medicine for diarrhoea.
- Coir, which is fibre from the husk, is used for ropes, mats, brushes.
- Its leaves can be used for brooms and roofs, among other things.
- Coconut shells can be used for charcoal, bowls, and buttons for shirts made in Hawaii.

- Other uses include cosmetics, oil, diesel, jelly, wax, wine, shoe polish, sponges and decorations, among many others.

In fact, the Maldives lists the Palm tree as its only natural resource.

One major attribute of the palm tree is its ability to withstand the strongest of storms – even hurricanes. It is flexible, and will often bend with the storm. The palm tree can bend parallel to the ground without breaking. Even though it doesn't have deep roots, it bounces back even stronger after the storm.

How is it that the palm tree is able to with stand such ferocious storms? How is the palm tree able to survive in conditions that have no nutrients, such as sand in the desert or sand on the sea front? How is it able to use its meagre resources to produce the largest seed in the plant kingdom?

It is because of its process.

Its process is the most profound thing I have ever come across in just about any specie in the plant kingdom.

The growth process of the palm tree is not like the grass that can happen overnight or in one season. First, it grows leaves, sending them on tall stalks towards the forest canopy. This juvenile stage may take decades. When it reaches adulthood, the tree starts to grow a trunk.

It has few roots. An abundance of thin roots grow outward from the plant, near the surface. Only a few of the roots penetrate deep into the soil.

Its first fruit usually comes in 5-6 years, and it takes 15-20 years to reach peak production. Compared to grass and a few other plants, this is a very long process.

The leaves of the palm tree barely have nutrients; they hold only a third of the nutrients of what other plants hold. But where this may seem like a bad thing, this lack of nutrients works in its favour, because its leaves don't get eaten by insects and nibbling animals.

And the palm tree has no branches. It doesn't expend its nutrients on diverse branches, but remains contained, having a single-minded focus on its growth. This also allows it to stay flexible in the face of a storm with nothing weighing it down.

One phenomenal thing about the palm tree is how it is able to flourish even though it is located in sand that has no nutrients and not soil. The palm tree's water-recycling system is amazing. Its unique architecture – the shape of the leaves at the top of the tree – acts as a funnel. During a rainstorm, these leaves collect nutrients and water and funnel them back to the roots. By the time the water gets to the base of the tree, it is no longer just rain water, because it would have collected nutrients from the droppings of lizards, snails and other birds that live on it.

Researchers have found that when it rains, almost all the rainwater ends up less than a meter from its base and it is full of nutrients. This is more than three times the amount of nutrients found in soils around other plants.

How does this apply to you?

i. Like the Palm tree, it is important to take your time to go through your process, no matter how much time it seems to be taking.
ii. Use what is meant to kill you – storms, insects and birds – to your advantage.
iii. The Palm tree focuses its nutrients on growing the largest seed in the plant kingdom, not the largest leaves in the plant kingdom. This is

        important because leaves can be attacked and eaten by insects, while seeds remain hidden while they develop.
- iv. Invest your resources on your "seed": your purpose and your vision. Do not invest your resources on unimportant things that other people will see, like money and material things.
- v. Cut off every unnecessary thing in your life, like the Palm tree that has no branches, and use your meagre resources to flourish.
- vi. Like the Palm tree, do not grow deep roots on this earth where things perish, focus on growing upwards towards Jesus.

I hope you choose to embrace your process and flourish like the Palm tree.

Heather Lindsey uses an analogy of an Elephant and a dog in her book, The Purpose Room.

The dog gives birth to a litter of puppies every three months, but it takes an elephant five years to birth just one elephant. Dogs are small, and have shorter lifespans – an average of twenty years – in comparison to the massive size of the elephant, which can live for seventy years. The elephant is birthing something huge and that is why it takes more time. Do not compare your process with another person's process.

I went through my own process in life.

I went through diverse challenges.

Sometimes I thought I couldn't take it anymore. Many times I thought I had made a mistake, and felt like giving up. Many times, I was depressed.

But the process didn't kill me. It made me stronger. It developed my character. It built muscles for greatness in me.

No amount of money in this world can buy the experiences I have gone through. No amount of money can replace the intimate relationship I have developed with my Father, Jesus and the Holy Spirit.

No amount of money could have bought the influence, the lives that have been touched and the impact here on earth and eternity, and this is only the beginning.

Nothing in this world could have restored my marriage and my family like God has done.

I am no longer trying to become a rich woman; instead, I am becoming THE RICHER WOMAN.

I hope you choose to become THE RICHER WOMAN.

# Acknowledgements

First of all, I would like to thank my Father in Heaven, God, my Saviour and Lord, Jesus, and my friend and helper, the Holy Spirit. This book is Your book. I couldn't have done it without You. You gave the vision and made provision. When the idea to write the book came I didn't think it was possible but Lord, You encouraged me to just start. You led me each step of the way, You redirected me when I started writing about something totally different. When I was afraid of being so open and what people would think, You encouraged me. When I was considering not being obedient, You warned me. When I got distracted and procrastinated, You put me back on track. You gave me strength when the enemy tried to attack and distract me. When I needed support, You sent me encouragers, prayer partners and accountability partners. I am forever indebted to You, Father. I will serve You all the days of my life. You gave me beauty for ashes. You turned my life around and made me a shining star. You were with me in my most difficult times. You have always been with me and I am eternally grateful. I am absolutely nothing without You and all that I am is because of You. Thank You for the privilege and honour of being a part of this book, of joining You at work. Who am I that you are mindful of me? Just a broken vessel that You didn't reject, but instead You chose to restore and to use mightily for Your Glory. I love You.

I would like to thank my husband, John Olugbenga Oshikoya. You are the bone of my bone. You were made for me. I wouldn't be who I am without you. Thank you for loving me just as Christ loves the church. Thank you for being patient with me and never giving up on me. Thank you for holding me up, as broken as I was. Thank you for believing in me. Thank you for being the best husband anyone could ever ask for. Thank you for being a wonderful father to our children. Thank you for forgiving me when I caused you great despair. Thank you for being a role model to so many. Thank you for loving me despite my many flaws. Your love is the epitome of 'The Redeeming love'. I see Jesus in you. Thank you for everything. Thank you for being 'The Richer Man'. I love you eternally.

To my children, Oluwaferanmi, Oluwafiorehanmi, Olaoluwaloseyi, thank you for bringing colour into my life. I am so privileged to be your mother. You make me so proud. Thank you for being patient with me even with my flaws and especially when I have to be away working. Thank you for being "The Richer Kids"I love you.

To my parents. Daddy, I love you very much and I thank God for you. Thank you for always listening to me and always supporting me. Thank you for teaching me never to give up in adversity and never to comprise on my God-given values. I thank God that you and mummy stayed together, my children are benefitting from this sacrifice. Mummy, you are the strongest woman that I know. I love you from the bottom of my heart. Thank you for doing everything to make sure we had what we needed growing up, even though you were constrained. Thank you for beating brain tumour's three times. I'm the mother I am because of you.

Brother Seun and Wonu, thank you for loving me despite my flaws. I thank God for our new journey. I love you both.

Mayode, my brother and my best friend. Oh how I love you. The love I have for you has no boundaries and no limitations. You are my younger brother but more often than not you have acted as my older brother. Thank you for being there for me when I was going through my own process, you gave your all so that I won't lack. I love you and Damilola dearly.

Fade and Aunty Lola, I consider you both my sister and my mum respectively. I love you both. Aunty Lola you are a pillar to the entire Aboderin family. Thank you for everything, for being there for us even in our tough times. Fade, you are not just my sister but my spiritual mentor. You have been a blessing to me and my nuclear family. I am eternally grateful.

Pastor Wale Adefarasin, I love you like I love my earthly father. You have been a father to me in so many ways. Thank you for being a light in the midst of darkness. Thank you for being a true example of Jesus. I'm grateful for you and Pastor Laolu.

Pastor Sola and Pastor Bimbo Fola Alade, thank you for your support in this journey, especially your words of encouragement, advice and prayers. Gbenga and I are eternally grateful.

To my Oshikoya family, Mummy and Daddy and siblings, most especially Sister Feyi, thank you for being so gracious to me and loving me like a sister and child.

Our brother and sister Jola and Babasola, thank you for being there for us over the years and introducing Gbenga and I to each other.

My aunties and Uncles, Aunty Gbemi, Aunty Kemi, Uncle Dolapo, etc. My cousins Ayomide, Damola, Ebun, Fara, Ari, Funmi, Jide and everyone, thank you. I love you.

My coach and spiritual father, Lanre Olusola, thank you for being the best coach in the world and for supporting me and providing me with a platform to soar. Coach Lilian Adegbola, thank you for all your support.

Pastor Demola Ademuson, Sister Sherry, Pastor Odunrinde, Pastor Bolarinwa Akinlabi, Pastor Tunde Usidame, thank you for encouraging me in my journey of faith and for all your prayers & encouragement.

Omotayo Adeola, where do I start from? You are God sent. Thank you for the sleepless nights and time without asking for anything in return. The editing process though long, was impactful even to me. It was a process of healing. You also coached me and encouraged me whenever I wanted to give up. You are the younger sister that I always longed for.

My sisters and best friends, Wunmi and Tola. Thank you for being my sisters. You both have been with me through some of the toughest challenges in my life and also celebrated with me. I'm eternally grateful.

My prayer partners and sisters, Teni Giwa-Osagie, Foluso Gbadamosi, Tolu Kasali, Esther Longe, Dupe Emmanuel, Teju Abisoye, Toju Olaitan and Bimbo Smith. Thank you for praying with me through these last few years. Thank you for all your advice and for keeping me accountable and ensuring I finish this book.

My dream team, Oyakhire Russel, Shola Ajayi, my mentees and the DIA team members, Kanyin Adio-Moses, Ruth Zubairu, Bisola Soneye, Hilary Taiwo, Simisola Agunbiade, Raquel Jacobs, Eva Akaakar, Gbeke Osinowo and all my other mentees. Thank you for being a blessing to me and helping me with God's purpose and vision.

My soul sisters, Debo, Shiyan, Nnenna, Funke, Funmi, Tayo, Yewande, Bunmi and my sister friends Taiwo

Akintokun, Kehinde Adewole, Timi Ejiwunmi. Thank you for your love, friendship and support in this journey of life.

Uche Pedro and the entire Bella Naija Team, Bukky Karibi Whtye and the entire Invicta Africa team. Thank you from the bottom of my heart for all your support from inception.

My Ignite youth ministers and Ignite members, thank you for all your prayers.

To everyone who has attended my events, sponsored my events, encouraged me on social media, prayed for me, supported me, thank you.

To every character that played a part in this book, thank you. God is intentional and He makes ALL things beautiful. Without you this story won't be complete.

# About the Author

The Father's daughter, Omilola Oshikoya is a wife to her best friend, John Olugbenga Oshikoya. They have been married for over 10 years and are blessed with three amazing children.

She is Africa's Premier Wealth Coach with over 13 years' experience in finance & investment banking. Omilola's goal is to inspire this generation to live the Richer™ Life and to help create wealth and eradicate poverty in Africa through a tool she created called "The Hand of Wealth" which focuses on five areas: What true wealth is, How to create wealth (business/entrepreneurship), How to manage wealth, How to grow wealth (personal finance) & How to use wealth.

Omilola is the founder of Omilola Oshikoya International (OOI), a life & finance coaching company. In 2015, OOI held its first conference called the "Do It Afraid" Conference at the Civic Centre, Lagos. The theme was "A moth or a butterfly which would you rather be? In 2016, OOI held its first entrepreneurship workshop, with the theme, "Agribusiness: The Next Frontier." The workshop aimed to showcase the business opportunities in agribusiness in Nigeria. The second "Do It Afraid" conference held in December 2016 and the theme was "The flourishing palm tree and its process." OOI held its first international event in London, in 2017.

Omilola is a contributor to "The Money Book" and the author of "The Richer Woman." She is also a co-host for a talk show titled, "The Heart of the Matter", which airs in 44 African Countries including the United Kingdom.

Omilola was listed among the YNaija & Leading Ladies Africa 100 most inspiring women in Nigeria in 2016. She was also a mentor under the Tony Elumelu Entrepreneurship program and was an independent monitor under the Youth Enterprise with the Innovation in Nigeria Programme.

In 2016, Omilola was given an award by the Lagos State University Students' Union in recognition of her immense contribution to Youth & National Development. In 2014, Omilola was recognized as a Chosen Youth by the La Roche Leadership Foundation, founded by the Executive Governor of Lagos State, His Excellency Akinwunmi Ambode, and given an award for exemplary leadership attributes as a Youth, and contributing to the sustainable development of the larger society.

She has been invited to speak at companies such as Google, Ericsson Nigeria, Accenture, Total Nigeria Plc, Access Bank Plc, among others.

She has also been interviewed by the major Newspapers, and as a speaker, she has been invited to speak at high profile events and several talk shows on television and radio. She has been featured on international platforms such as BBC Africa and the Huffington Post. She has also been invited to speak at churches, conferences and other events.

Previously, Omilola worked as the Head of Media and Publications at Guiding Light Assembly. She set up the church's social media accounts, developed and revised the church website and was responsible for all publications, publicity and communications of the church office.

With over 10 years' work experience in Finance and Accounting, Omilola has garnered experience as a seasoned Financial Analyst covering areas such as Fund Management,

Infrastructure/Project Finance, Corporate Finance, Financial Advisory, Project Management, Internal Control Analysis and Audit. She was an Associate in ARM Investment Managers, where she worked in areas such as Infrastructure Finance, Investment Banking/Financial Advisory and the ARM Hospitality and Retail Fund. Among her notable achievements while serving in this role are the start-up of a US$250 million Hospitality and Retail fund, achieving first financial close at US$31million, and the launch of the Fund's flagship project, an internationally branded Four Star hotel in Victoria Island, Lagos. She also negotiated a concession agreement and structured equity for a US$6.5million Urban Infrastructure Parking Project with Nigerian State Government under a Public-Private-Partnership scheme, and managed a US$14 million Bombardier Lear Jet 45XR asset.

Omilola's other work experience includes The Royal Bank of Scotland (UK), Akintola Williams Deloitte, and FutureView Financial Services Ltd, where she worked in the corporate finance division.

Omilola has a BA in Accounting and Finance from the University of Kent (UK). She obtained a certificate in latest techniques and software for performing Hotel market studies and valuations from the School of Hospitality Management, PennState University, Pennsylvania, USA.

She is a NCFE UK certified life coach, she has attended various conferences worldwide, including the 2010 Annual Nigeria Energy & Power Summit (NEPS) Abuja, the 2011 Arabian Hotel Investment Conference UAE, and the 2011 Tourism and Infrastructure Investment Summit & Awards, South Africa.

Omilola is an ordained youth minister at Ignite, the youth ministry of Guiding Light Assembly.

Made in the USA
Lexington, KY
27 April 2017